IMPROVE
PRONUNCIATION

and learn over 500 commonly mispronounced words

This book will hopefully be of help to anyone who struggles with learning English.

© JAKUB MARIAN, 2013

ISBN-13: 978-1492192855

First Edition, August 2013

Author and Publisher:

Jakub Marian

Sewanstraße 217

10319 Berlin

Germany

www.jakubmarian.com

Printed by:

On-Demand Publishing LLC

100 Enterprise Way

Suite A200

Scotts Valley, CA 95066

USA

Before you start reading

If you happen to have found this book freely available on the Internet (from an illegal source), please consider buying a legal copy (there is a PDF, Kindle, and Paperback edition) which is also the only one guaranteed to be up to date. An electronic version of this book can be obtained for $4.99 or less. You can find links to all the versions at

http://jakubmarian.com/pronunciation/

If you have bought this book, you could be interested in the fact that you can also buy an electronic gift version for your friends under the given URL.

As for the **licence for the paperback edition**—you can make as many physical or electronic copies as you wish and share them with the members of your household. You can convert the book to any format you wish for your personal use. However, if you want to give a copy to a friend (or generally someone not within your household), you are required to buy another copy (there is also an electronic gift copy available). You are not allowed to share the book publicly in any way.

*If you find any **error** in the book, be it a factual or grammatical error, a typo, or a formatting issue, please send me an email to*

jakub.marian@gmail.com

with the subject "English pronunciation" containing a description of the error, so that it can be fixed in the next edition.

What to expect from this book

The first part of this book is concerned with words that are most commonly pronounced wrong by English learners. Pronunciation is written using the International Phonetic Alphabet (IPA), which is standard among contemporary English dictionaries, and using a pseudo-English notation that uses just four IPA characters (ə, æ, ʌ, and ð).

If you can't read IPA yet, don't worry; getting used to the pseudo-English notation will be just a matter of minutes (the rules will be explained at the beginning of the first chapter), and you will be able to read most of it right away. The list of words looks like this:

height [haɪt] (**haayt**); the pronunciation is as if it were written "hight". The "e" is there just to confuse foreigners.

wolf [wʊlf] (**woolf**); this is one of a few words in which a single "o" is pronounced as [ʊ] (as "oo" in "good"). Other examples include **woman** [ˈwʊmən] (**woo**-mən), and similar words **womb** [wuːm] (**woom**), the organ in which a child before birth is, and **tomb** [tuːm] (**toom**), a place in which remains of dead people are stored. **Tombstone** is pronounced "**toom**-stone".

Greenwich [ˈɡrɛnɪtʃ] (**gren**-itch) or [ˈɡrɪnɪdʒ] (**grin**-idzh); you probably know this word from the Greenwich Mean Time (GMT) standard. Just remember that there is no green witch in Greenwich.

colonel [ˈkʰɜːnᵊl] (**kə'ə**-nl) UK, [ˈkʰɝːnᵊl] (**kər**-nl) US; is there a kernel inside a colonel (a military officer)? Well, at least in pronunciation, there is (they are pronounced the same).

After finishing the first part of this book, you will have learned more than **300 such words**.

In the second part of this book, you will learn about the most common patterns of errors in English. You will learn that "eu" in English is usually pronounced [juː] (yoo) or [uː] (oo) (as in **neutral** = "**n(y)oo**-trəl"), that "x" at the beginning of a word is pronounced as [z] (as in **Xerox** = "**zee**-roks"), and several dozen more such rules.

There's also a list of words in which "o" is pronounced as [ʌ] (as in "come") which learners often mistakenly pronounce as [o] (there are about **40 such common words**). For example:

> **front** [frʌnt] (**frʌnt**)
>
> **onion** [ˈʌnjən] (**ʌn-yən**)
>
> **won** [ˈwʌn] (**wʌn**)

You will also learn about words that can be pronounced in two different ways such as "**wind**":

(NOUN) [wɪnd] (**win'd**) is a movement of air (it can also be a verb meaning "to blow to a wind instrument").

(VERB) [waɪnd] (**waaynd**) means "to turn, especially something around something else". For example, a river or a way can "waaynd", or you can "waaynd" a wire around a coil.

Many such words differ only in stress position, for example:

conserve; [kənˈsɜːv] (**kən-sə'əv**) UK, [kənˈsɝːv] (**kən-sərv**) US (VERB) means "to use as little as possible" (e.g. "to conserve energy") or "to protect something from being destroyed" (e.g. "to conserve wildlife"); [ˈkɒnsɜːv] (**konn-sə'əv**) UK, [ˈkɑːnsɝːv] (**kaan-sərv**) US (NOUN) is synonymous to "whole fruit jam". Unlike in other languages, it *isn't* synonymous to a can (an aluminium container).

Finally, in the third part of this book, you will learn the International Phonetic Alphabet (IPA) and basics of English phonology.

TABLE OF CONTENTS

FOREWORD

This foreword explains why I believe that English is a hard language to learn. If you are eager to start improving your pronunciation, just skip to the next section.

What is it that makes English so hard for foreigners to learn? I believe that it is a combination of its spelling and pronunciation. Most languages have a regulatory body which issues spelling reforms as the pronunciation of the language develops. On the other hand, English spelling is "regulated" by influential dictionaries, such as Webster's dictionary or The Oxford English Dictionary.

By the time these dictionaries were written (during the 19th century), English pronunciation had already been changing for several hundred years. This was unfortunately not reflected by the authors of the dictionaries, and, in addition to that, English pronunciation has diverged even further from its spelling since the first editions of these dictionaries were written. As a result, English spelling has become very irregular.

This poses a much greater problem to learners of English than to native speakers, because native speakers know how to pronounce words; they just have to be able to spell them correctly, which is not such a big problem nowadays when anyone can use a spell checker.

Learners of English, on the contrary, meet most of their vocabulary in written form first. It is often possible (and even appropriate) to derive the meaning of a new word from the context, but instead of looking up the correct pronunciation in a dictionary, learners tend to guess what the pronunciation might be (according to their experience) and then use this pronunciation internally when thinking about the word. Unfortunately, such guesses are wrong most of the time.

One of the reasons they are wrong so often is an unusually large number of vowels and consonants present in English which must be distinguished in order to be understood correctly (the so called "minimal pairs") which sound almost the same to the learner's ear.

For example, none of the words "bed", "bet", "bad", "bat", "bud", and "but" is pronounced the same as any of the others (they are pronounced, in the same order: [bɛd], [bɛt], [bæd], [bæt], [bʌd], and [bʌt]). Nevertheless, these are all patterns that can be learned (and you will do so in Part III of this book), because all the differences are indicated in spelling in quite a regular way.

A much greater problem is posed by spelling ambiguities and historical spellings that don't follow current pronunciation rules at all. Why is "dear" pronounced the same as "deer" but "bear" and "beer" sound different? Or why is "colonel" pronounced the same as "kernel"?

In addition to the problems we have already mentioned, there is no indication of stress placement in English whatsoever. In most languages, stress placement is governed by relatively simple rules; in English, it is almost completely irregular (apart from a few hard-to-follow patterns), and words can even change their meaning depending on stress position. Also, pronunciation of vowels usually changes depending on whether they are stressed. For example, "angel" is pronounced ['eɪndʒəl] (**eyn**-dzhəl) whereas "angelic" is pronounced [ænˈdʒɛlɪk] (æn-**dzhel**-ik), i.e. not only has the stress shifted by adding a suffix, but also the pronunciation of both of the vowels has changed (we will see several such words in the list).

In terms of vocabulary, English is like a patchwork. It is a mixture of (mostly) Middle French, Anglo-Saxon, Latin, and Greek. As a result, there are often different words to express the same idea. For example, one doesn't speak of "touchy feedback" but of "tactile feedback", and not of "smelly system" but of "olfactory system" (the system in the body that perceives smells). If you do something using your hands, you don't do it "handily", you do it "manually", and the "green" electricity you may be using doesn't come from "sunny plants" but from "solar plants".

This process results in an amount of vocabulary that is somewhat larger than necessary. This is not a bad thing *per se*; it adds some expressive power to English and makes it a good starting point for learning other European languages. In combination with English pronunciation and spelling problems, this can, however, be a huge nuisance to learners, especially since English spelling of such words usually reflects the original spelling in the language of origin, not its contemporary English pronunciation.

Even though learning English in general requires a substantial amount of time and dedication, I believe that after you finish reading this book, you should be able to cope at least with all the problems mentioned above. I hope that you will also enjoy doing so.

Jakub Marian
Berlin, 2013

PART I

MISPRONOUNCED WORDS

I.1 INTRODUCTION

This chapter forms the core of this book. Even though there are rules and patterns for English pronunciation that can be learned (this is what especially Part III of this book is about), there are many words whose pronunciation has to be learned by heart.

In the first part of this book, we shall take a look at words which a majority of English learners pronounce wrong at some point in their "career" as English speakers. The words are ordered so that the most common words come first, the least common last.

If you don't like lengthy introductions, you can skip to the next section and start reading the words right away (you will probably do just fine). If you are interested in basic conventions used in the rest of this book, just read further.

The IPA transcription used in this book is very precise (it is always written in square brackets); it distinguishes, for example [e] and [ɛ], [a] and [ɑ] etc. Also, [ʰ] denotes an aspirated consonant (a consonant after which a slight shade of "h" is pronounced); this is usually ignored by dictionaries to maintain simplicity. [ʳ] is used for British English and is pronounced as [r] if the following word begins with a vowel. Short [i] after [r] usually sounds more like [ɪ], but it is traditional to denote it also as [i], and this book follows this convention. The full IPA for English is described in Part III.

If you already know some IPA, reading the book may actually be a good way to master it really well. If you don't know any IPA yet, you can read the pseudo-English transcription. In order to do so, you will have to remember just four IPA characters; the rest should be pronounced as you would intuitively pronounce it as an English word. The characters you have to remember are:

[ə] is pronounced as "a" in "a book" (i.e. as the indefinite article). It is a neutral sound, as if you were just releasing air through your vocal chords. If you sometimes think that there's an "ə" used in a place where you would expect "i" as in "pit" (or conversely), don't worry; these two sounds are often interchangeable.

[æ] is a sound approximately between "a" in "father" and "e" in "bed". The symbol is used to remind you that English "a" (as in "cat" = "kæt", "bad" = "bæd", "sad" = "sæd" etc.) is pronounced somewhat differently than you are used from your mother tongue.

[ʌ] is the sound of "u" in "but" (bʌt) and "o" in "come" (kʌm).

[ð] is the sound of "th" in "that" or "father". It is produced by saying "d" but putting the tip of your tongue on the back of your upper teeth instead of the fleshy part behind it.

There are also a few groups of letters used consistently in the pseudo-English notation (but don't worry about them too much; you will remember them naturally as you start reading the list): "*aw*" is pronounced as in "l*aw*", "*oo*" as in "c*oo*l", "*oo*" (italicised) as in "g*oo*d" (the same as "u" in "put"), "*ee*" (italicised) is used to denote the same sound as in "s*ee*" but short, and "*oh*" is used to denote [oʊ] which is how Americans pronounce "oh"; in British English, "oh" is pronounced as "əu".

The pseudo-English notation uses dashes to divide each word into simpler parts, for example "police" = "pə-**lees**". The stressed part is bold (if the word is monosyllabic, then it may be bold just to draw attention to the pronunciation). These parts often correspond to the syllables of the word, but they do not if this could lead to a wrong pronunciation, so don't pronounce the dashes as any kind of pause. For example "recipe" is denoted as "**res**-ip-*ee*", although the syllables are in fact "res-i-pee", but this would mislead some people to pronounce the "i" as "**aay**".

If the American pronunciation differs from the British one, the one just explained is marked by the symbol UK or US after the given pronunciation. If several variants are given but neither of the two symbols is present, then they are all in use both in British English as well as in American English.

1.2 WORDS YOU DEFINITELY *SHOULD* KNOW

This section contains words that are common in everyday spoken language and should be mastered by all English learners.

height [haɪt] (**haayt**); the pronunciation is as if it were written "hight". The "e" is there just to confuse foreigners.

fruit [fruːt] (**froot**); a similar situation as in the previous word; simply ignore the "i".

suit [suːt] (**soot**), in the UK also [sjuːt] (**syoot**); as in the case of "fruit", the "i" is silent.

since [sɪns] (**sins**); some people, misled by the "e" at the end, pronounced this word as "**saayns**".

subtle [ˈsʌtʰl] (**sʌ**-tl) UK, [ˈsʌɾl] (**sʌ**-dl) US; "btle" simply doesn't sound good. Don't pronounce the "b".

queue [kʰjuː] (**kyoo**); if you want to pronounce this word correctly, just think of the Q at the beginning; "ueue" is not pronounced at all.

change [tʃeɪndʒ] (**tcheyndzh**); the word is pronounced with "ey", not with "æ" or "e".

hotel [həʊˈtʰɛl] (həʊ-**tel**) UK, [hoʊˈtʰɛl] (hoh-**tel**) US; "ho ho *ho, tell* me why you are not at home" is something Santa Claus could ask you if you stayed in a hotel over Christmas. It is most certainly not the reason why it is called "hotel", but it will hopefully help you remember that the stress is actually on the second syllable (there is not [tl] at the end).

recipe ['rɛsɪpi] (**res**-ip-ee); "cipe" in this case doesn't rhyme with "ripe"; it consists of two separate syllables.

iron ['aɪən] (**aay**-ən) UK, ['aɪɚn] (**aay**-rn) US; this word is mispronounced by almost 100% of beginning English learners who pronounce it as **aay**-rən or **aay**-ron, but none of these pronunciations is correct. The same is true also for "ironed" ['aɪənd] (**aay**-ənd) UK, ['aɪɚnd] (**aay**-rn'd) US and "ironing" ['aɪənɪŋ] (**aay**-ə-ning) UK, ['aɪɚnɪŋ] (**aay**-ər-ning) US.

lettuce ['lɛtɪs] (**let**-is) UK, ['lɛɾɪs] (**led**-is) US; remember that lettuce doesn't grow on a spruce; and it also doesn't rhyme with it.

womb [wuːm] (**woom**), **tomb** [tʰuːm] (**toom**); people tend to pronounce "o" as in "lot". Think about "tomb" as about "to"+"mb". "Mb" may sound nice in Swahili, but not so much in English, so the "b" is silent. The same applies to all other words in which "m" and "b" belong to the same syllable, such as **numb** [nʌm] (**nʌm**) and **plumb** [pʰlʌm] (**plʌm**). The "b" is silent even in "number" when it means "more numb" and in "plumber".

comb [kəʊm] (**kəum**) UK, [koʊm] (**koh'm**) US; the toothed device used for styling hair is pronounced without the "b" at the end. Remember: the "m" already looks like a comb, so no "b" is needed.

bomb [bɒm] (**bom**) UK, [bɑːm] (**baam**) US; after all the other words, it shouldn't surprise you that the "b" is silent. This word is perhaps even more confusing than the others in that it also exists in most other languages in the same written form but with the "b" pronounced. The same pronunciation is used also for **bombing** ['bɒmɪŋ] (**bom**-ing) UK, ['bɑːmɪŋ] (**baam**-ing) US.

climb [klaɪm] (**klaaym**); as in the previous words, the "b" in "mb" is silent. This is true also for "climbing" ['klaɪmɪŋ] (**klaay**-ming), "climbed" [ˈklaɪmd] (klaaymd), and "climber" [ˈklaɪməʳ] (**klaay**-mə) UK, [ˈklaɪmɚ] (**klaay**-mr) US.

comfortable [ˈkʰʌmfətəbᵊl] (**kʌm**-fə-tə-bl) UK, in the US also [ˈkʰʌmftəbᵊl] (**kʌm**-ftə-bl); if you "come for a table" to a furniture shop, it will hopefully be comfortable, although it doesn't rhyme with it.

Greenwich [ˈgrɛnɪtʃ] (**gren**-itch) or [ˈgrɪnɪdʒ] (**grin**-idzh); you probably know this word from the Greenwich Mean Time (GMT) standard. Just remember that there is no green witch in Greenwich.

elite [ɪˈliːt] (ih-**leet**), sometimes also [eɪˈliːt] (ey-**leet**); elite people are certainly not a "lite version" of the population. Don't rhyme them with it.

bear [bɛəʳ] (**beə**) UK, [bɛr] (**ber**) US,
pear [pʰɛəʳ] (**peə**) UK, [pʰɛr] (**per**) US,
wear [wɛəʳ] (**weə**) UK, [wɛr] (**wer**) US; the animal, the fruit, and what we do with clothes—all of them are pronounced with the [ɛ] (**e**) sound. In other words, if you've heard a story about someone's grandpa being attacked by a beer while eating his peer, you can be pretty sure the storyteller hadn't read this book.

tear; this word may cause some confusion, because it has two completely unrelated meanings. When it denotes a water drop coming out of someone's eye, it's pronounced [tʰɪəʳ] (**ti'ə**) UK or [tʰɪr] US (**tir**). When it denotes the process of "ripping" something, it is pronounced [tɛəʳ] (**teə**) UK or [tɛr] (**ter**) US.

weight [weɪt] (**weyt**); those who realize that "height" is correctly pronounced [haɪt] (**haayt**) sometimes tend to mistakenly pronounce "weight" the same as "white".

pour [pʰɔːʳ] (**paw**) UK, [pʰɔːr] (**paw'r**) or [pʰoʊr] (**poh'r**) US; although the word looks like having a French origin and "ou" in French words is usually pronounced [uː] (e.g. route [ruːt] (root)), in this case the origin is not French, and so is not the pronunciation. On the other hand, the word "poor" can be pronounced either with [ʊ] (**oo**) or with [ɔː] (**aw**) (both are equally valid). If you use the former, you can remember not to use the "poor" pronunciation for "pour".

pyramid [ˈpʰɪrəmɪd] (**pir-ə-mid**); the "pyr" in the word "pyramid" has nothing to do with the prefix "pyro-" which comes from Greek and is used in the word **pyromania** [ˌpaɪrəʊˈmeɪnɪə] (**paay-rəu-mei-nee-ə**) UK, [ˌpaɪroʊˈmeɪnɪə] (**paay-roh-mei-nee-ə**) US.

chose [tʃəʊz] (**tchəu'z**) UK, [tʃoʊz] (**tchoh'z**) US; the past tense of "**choose**" [tʃuːz] (**tchooz**) is sometimes wrongly pronounced the same as "choose", perhaps because it looks similar to **lose** [luːz] (**looz**).

grind [graɪnd] (**graaynd**); there are only 4 English words that end with "rind": rind, grind, regrind, and tamarind. Tamarind is a tree, and it is the only one of those in which "rind" is pronounced as one would expect: [rind]. In the other three, it is pronounced as [raɪnd] (**raaynd**). ("Rind" is the outer skin of some types of fruit, for example "lemon rind".)

steak [steɪk] (**steyk**),
break [breɪk] (**breyk**),
great [greɪt] (**greyt**); the only three English words in which "ea" is pronounced as [eɪ] (**ey**). "Steak" is pronounced exactly the same as "stake", "break" as "brake", and "great" as "grate".

vinegar [ˈvɪnɪɡəʳ] (**vin-ig-ə**) UK, [ˈvɪnɪɡɚ] (**vin-ig-rr**) US is used to make food more **sour** [ˈsaʊəʳ] (**saau-ə**) UK, [ˈsaʊɚ] (**saau**-rr) US.

Although the word is related to **vine** [vaɪn] (vaayn), it is not pronounced so. And when we are at it, don't confuse pronunciation of "vine" and "wine"; a "vine" is a plant on which grapes grow and is pronounced with "v" at the beginning (as in "very"), "wine" is the liquid you can make out of the grapes and is pronounced with "w" at the beginning (as in "wow").

wolf [wʊlf] (**woolf**); this is one of a few words in which a single "o" is pronounced as [ʊ] (as "oo" in "good"). Other examples include **woman** ['wʊmən] (**woo**-mən), and similar words **womb** [wuːm] (**woom**), the organ in which a child before birth is, and **tomb** [tuːm] (**toom**), a place in which remains of dead people are stored. "**Tombstone**" is pronounced "**toom**-stone".

alien ['eɪliən] (**ei**-li-ən); although a lion would certainly be an unwelcome alien at your home, don't pronounce them the same. Just remember that an alien is not your **ally** ['ælaɪ] (**æ**-laay).

bull [bʊl] (**bool**); some people pronounce the "u" wrongly as [ʌ], as in "cut", but it is the same "u" as in "put".

bullet ['bʊlɪt] (**boo**-lit); as in the previous case, "u" is pronounced as [ʊ] (oo).

ballet ['bæleɪ] (**bæ**-lei) UK, [bæˈleɪ] (bæ-**lei**) US; somewhat surprisingly, the final "t" remains silent.

scene [siːn] (**seen**); "sc" in this word is pronounced just as [s]. The same is true also for "**scenario**" [sɛˈnɑːriəʊ] (se-**naa**-ri-əu) UK, [sɪˈnæriəʊ] (si-**næ**-ri-oh) US.

muscle ['mʌsl] (**mʌ**-sl); another word in which "sc" is pronounced just as "s".

walk [wɔːk] (**waw'k**) UK, [wɑːk] (**waak**) US,

chalk, [tʃɔːk] (**tchaw'k**) UK, [tʃɑːk] (**tchaak**) US,

talk [tʰɔːk] (**taw'k**) UK, [tɑːk] (**taak**) US; both in standard American and British English, the "l" remains silent (but it modifies the pronunciation of "a" in front of it). There exist, however, also dialects in which it is pronounced.

calm [kʰɑːm] (**kaam**); **palm** [pʰɑːm] (**paam**); English doesn't seem to like the combination "alm", so the "l" remains silent in most dialects (however, there are some American ones in which it is pronounced).

almond ['ɑːmənd] (**aa-mənd**) UK, ['amənd] (**aa-mənd**), ['almənd] (**aal-mənd**), or ['æmənd] (**æm-ənd**) US; the "l" remains silent in most dialects.

salmon ['sæmən] (**sæ-mən**); there's something fishy about this word. Perhaps the pronunciation.

calf, [kʰɑːf] (**kaaf**) UK, [kʰæf] (**kæf**) US; **half** [hɑːf] (**haaf**) UK, [hæf] (**hæf**) US; as above, the "l" is silent.

salt [sɔːlt] (**saw'lt**); after all the silent "l"s, one could get an impression that it is silent all the time, but the "l" in "salt" is pronounced.

folk [fəʊkʰ] (**fəu'k**) [foʊk] (**foh'k**); and again one of the words in which "l" is silent (in most dialects).

pudding ['pʊdɪŋ] (**poo**-ding); if you drop a bowl of pudding, it forms a puddle [pʌdl] (with "pʌd"), but when it is still in the bowl, it is, well, with "poo".

target [ˈtʰɑːgɪt] (**taag**-it) UK, [ˈtɑːrgɪt] (**taarg**-it) US; it would certainly be possible to "get some tar" in order to mark a target. Although "target" is etymologically related neither to "tar" nor to "get", it is a way to remember that the "g" is as in "get", not as "j" as in "jet".

sandwich [ˈsænwɪtʃ] (**san**-witch) or [ˈsænwɪdʒ] (**san**-widzh); would you like to eat a sandwich with sand? If you wouldn't, don't pronounce the "d".

caffeine [ˈkʰæfiːn] (**kæ**-feen) is, after all, in coffee, so it would be more logical to call it "coffeen", wouldn't it? As a compromise between the two, at least "ei" is pronounced as "ee".

angel [ˈeɪndʒəl] (**eyn**-dzhəl); unlike many other words beginning with "ang-" such as "angle" [ˈæŋgl] (**æng**-gl), "angel" is pronounced with [eɪndʒ] (eyndzh) at the beginning.

angelic [ænˈdʒɛlɪk] (æn-**dzhe**-lik); although it is derived from "angel", the stress has moved to the second syllable and the vowels have to be changed accordingly.

sweat [swɛt] (**swet**); have you ever tasted sweat? It's not exactly sweet. Don't pronounce it this way.

bury [ˈbɛri] (**ber**-ri); a **burial** [ˈbɛriəl] (**ber**-ri-əl) is a sad and important event. Don't spoil it by pronouncing it wrong. It is pronounced exactly the same as "berry" (i.e. there is no "uh" or "ʌ" sound).

xenon [ˈzɛnɒn] (**zen**-on) UK, [ˈziːnɑn] (**zee**-naan) US,
xerox [ˈzɪərɒks] (**zi**-ə-roks) UK, [ˈzɪrɑːks] (**zi**-raaks) US,
xenophobia [ˌzɛnəˈfəʊbiə] (zen-ə-**fəu**-bee-ə) UK, [ˌzɛnəˈfoʊbiə] (ze-nə-**foh**-bee-ə) or [ˌzinəˈfoʊbiə] (zee-nə-**foh**-bee-ə) US; perhaps as a

great disappointment to all fans of a dubbed version of Xena: Warrior Princess comes the fact that "x" at the beginning of any word is not pronounced as [ks] but as [z].

anchor ['æŋkəʳ] (**æn**-kə) ['æŋkɚ] (**æn**-kr); although a ship that fishes for **anchovy** ['æntʃəvi] (**æn**-tchə-vee) UK, ['æntʃoʊvi] (**æn**-tchoh-vee) US will probably have an anchor, the two words are not etymologically related, and they are also pronounced differently.

gauge [geɪdʒ] (**geydzh**); this word is especially useful to guitarists who speak about string gauges (i.e. how thick they are). It is pronounced as if the "u" were not there.

draught [drɑːft] (**draaft**); this is just the British spelling of "draft", and is also pronounced the same. It is not spelled this way in all the meanings of "draft"; for example when it is a verb (i.e. when someone drafts something), it is spelled "draft" in British English as well.

chaos ['kʰeɪɒs] (**kei**-oss) UK, ['kʰeɪɑːs] (**kei**-aas) US; the pronunciation of this word is actually quite regular, but people tend to pronounce it as the same word in their own language, which usually differs from its English pronunciation.

infamous ['ɪnfəməs] (**in**-fə-məs); although the word is just "famous" with the prefix "in-" stuck in the front, it is not pronounced so.

niche [niːʃ] (**neesh**) UK, [nɪtʃ] (**nitch**) US; this word, originally meaning a shallow recess or simply a nice place or position, is also often used to mean a particular narrow field of interest (especially in business). Its pronunciation can be somewhat unexpected.

rhythm [ˈrɪðᵊm] (**ri-ðm**); there are only two common English words beginning with "rhy": "rhyme" and "rhythm" (if you don't count words derived from these), but "**rhyme**" is pronounced [raɪm] (**raaym**), so you cannot really say there is a rule for such words.

algorithm [ˈælgərɪðᵊm] (**æl-gə-ri-ðm**); the "rithm" part of "algorithm" is pronounced the same as "rhythm". Even though algorithm executes some operations in a certain "rhythm", the two words are in fact unrelated and the difference in spelling sometimes causes troubles to learners of English.

onion [ˈʌnjən] (**ʌn-yən**); one of a couple of words in which "o" is pronounced as [ʌ] (as in "come").

accessory [əkˈsɛsəri] (**ək-ses-ə-ree**); there is a common mispronunciation even among native speakers who sometimes pronounce it as [əˈsɛsəri] (**ə-ses-ə-ree**), without [k]. However, the [k] is there even in the original French word, and there is no reason not to say it also in English.

ion [ˈaɪɒn] (**aay**-on) or [ˈaɪən] (**aay**-ən) UK, [ˈaɪɑːn] (**aay**-aan) US is an atom or a molecule in which the total number of electrons is not equal to the total number of protons. Not to be confused with the name **Ian** pronounced [ˈiːən] (**ee**-ən).

cation [ˈkætaɪən] (**kæt**-aay-ən) or also [ˈkætˌaɪɑːn] (**kæt**-aay-aan) in the US is a positively charged **ion**, which therefore moves towards the **cat**hode; similarity with words like caution [ˈkʰɔːʃᵊn] (**kaw**-shn) UK, [ˈkʰɑːʃᵊn] (**kaa**-shn) US is only accidental.

hour [ˈaʊəʳ] (**aau**-ə) UK, [ˈaʊɚ] (**aau**-rr) US (both the same as "our"); the "h" at the beginning is silent, as it should be also in the name of the letter H [eɪdʒ] (**eydzh**). Some native speakers started to pronounce H as "heydzh" lately, but such pronunciation is regarded as uneducated by many. Other words with silent H at the beginning include:

honour ['ɒnəʳ] (**on**-ə) UK, honor ['ɑːnɚ] (**aan**-r) US; some learners mispronounce this word as if it had [ʌ] at the beginning.

honest ['ɒnɪst] (**on**-ist) UK, ['ɑːnɪst] (**aan**-ist) US; "hon" is pronounced exactly the same as in the previous word.

Hannah ['hɑnə] (**haa**-nə) UK, ['hænə] (**hæ**-nə) US; on the other hand, it is the last "h" that is silent in this name, not the first one.

ghetto ['gɛtəʊ] (**ge**-təu) UK, ['gɛtoʊ] (**ge**-to*h*) US; to end our discussion on silent "h", notice that it is also silent in "ghetto". Also, don't pronounce the "e" as [iː] (ee).

chocolate ['tʃɒklət] (**tchok**-lət) UK, ['tʃɑːklət] (**tchaak**-lət) or ['tʃɔːklət] (**tchaw'k**-lət) US; it's never too late for a piece of chocolate, but there's never "late" in the pronunciation of the word "chocolate".

(of) course [kʰɔːs] (**kaw's**) UK, [kʰɔːrs] (**kaw'rs**) or [kʰoʊrs] (**koh'rs**) US; although the word is of French origin, the "ou" is not pronounced as [uː] (oo) as is common in French words, but as [ɔː] (*aw*) or [oʊ] (as "o" in "go").

finance ['faɪnæns] (**faay**-næns) or [fəˈnæns] (fə-**næns**); just pay attention to the second vowel which is pronounced [æ], not [ə].

beige [beɪʒ] (**beyzh**); this word is of French origin and inherits its French pronunciation. The "g" is pronounced the same as in "massage".

garage is pronounced in the UK either as ['gærɑːʒ] (**gæ**-raazh) or ['gærɪdʒ] (**gæ**-ridzh), in the US it is usually [gəˈrɑːʒ] (gə-**raazh**).

photograph [ˈfəʊtəgrɑːf] (**fəu**-tə-graaf) UK, [ˈfoʊtəgræf] (**foh**-tə-græf) US; the word is synonymous to a photo, not the person who takes the photo as in many other languages. The person is a **photographer** [fəˈtɒgrəfəʳ] (fə-**togg**-rə-fə) UK, [fəˈtɑːgrəfɚ] (fə-**taag**-rə-fr) US; notice that the stress is now on the second syllable, whereas it was on the first syllable in "photograph". To make the confusion complete, the stress in the word **photographic** [ˌfəʊtəˈgræfɪk] (fəu-tə-**græf**-ik) UK, [ˌfoʊtəˈgræfɪk] (foh-tə-**græf**-ik) US is on the third syllable.

author [ˈɔːθəʳ] (**aw**-thə) UK, [ˈɔːθɚ] (**aw**-thr) US; this word exists in many languages, not just English. Notice that "th" is pronounced as [θ], i.e. not as in "that" [ðæt], but as in "think" [θɪŋk], and that "au" at the beginning is pronounced as [ɔː] (**aw**).

premiere [ˈprɛmɪɛə] (**pre**-mi-eə) UK, [prɪˈmɪr] (pri-**mir**) US; the American pronunciation can be somewhat surprising.

column [ˈkʰɒləm] (**koll**-əm) UK, [ˈkʰɑːləm] (**kaal**-əm) US; whether it is a column of text or a column in architecture, the pronunciation still retains some influence of its French origin. It is **not** [ʌ] as in **colour** [ˈkʰʌləʳ] (kʌ-lə), and there is also no [juː] (yoo) as in **volume** [ˈvɒljuːm] (**vol**-yoom) UK, [ˈvɑːljuːm] (**vaal**-yoom) US.

suite [swiːt] (**sweet**); meaning a set of rooms (in a hotel), a set of matching pieces of furniture, a certain type of musical composition, or a set of related computer programs, this word is pronounced exactly the same as "sweet".

genre [ˈʒɒ̃rə] or [ˈʒɒnrə] (**zhon**-rə) UK, [ˈʒɑːnɚ] (**zhaa**-nr) US; a very French word indeed. It is even pronounced with a nasal vowel in some variations of British English, i.e. with squeezing of the back of one's throat instead of saying [n].

debt [dɛt] (**det**); a word that has become abundant in media after the recent financial **crisis** [ˈkraɪsɪs] (**kraay**-sis). If you pronounce the "b", people will likely understand it as "dipped".

soccer [ˈsɒkəʳ] (**sokk**-ə) UK, [ˈsɑːkə-] (**saa**-kr) US; don't you dare say "soccer" outside of the US borders, unless you want to be ridiculed. "Soccer" is an American term for what is called "football" almost anywhere else (what Americans call just "football", is, in turn, usually called "American football" in the rest of the world). However, if you find it appropriate, don't pronounce it as **saucer** [ˈsɔːsəʳ] (**saw**-sə) UK, [ˈsɔːsə-] (**saw**-sr) US (a small plate).

sew [səʊ] (**səu**) UK, [soʊ] (**soh**) US; "to sew" means "to join (usually two pieces of textile) by stitches". The word **sewer** has two different meanings; if it is pronounced [ˈsəʊəʳ] (**səu**-ə) UK, resp. [ˈsoʊə-] (**soh**-rr) US, it is someone who sews (joins using stitches). If it is pronounced [ˈsuːəʳ] (**soo**-ə) UK or [ˈsuːə-] (**soo**-r) US, it is a pipe used to remove liquid human waste.

Linux [ˈlɪnəks] (**lin**-əks) or [ˈliːnʊks] (**lee**-nooks); one of the most popular operating systems on devices other than personal computers. It was created by Linus Torvalds; in honour of his name, never pronounce "Li" in "Linux" as "lie".

purchase [ˈpɜːtʃəs] (**pə'ə**-tchəs) UK, [ˈpɜˑtʃəs] (**pər**-tchəs) US; it is true that many people literally "chase discounts" when purchasing goods, but there is no "chase" in the pronunciation of "purchase".

worthy [ˈwɜːði] (**wə'ə**-ði) UK, [ˈwɜˑði] (**wər**-ði) US is pronounced with [ð], although "worth" is pronounced with [θ] (th).

schema [ˈskiːmə] (**skee**-mə); especially German speakers should pay attention here; "sch" is not pronounced as "sh" but as "sk". The same is true for **scheme** [skiːm] (skeem);

correct [kəˈrɛkt] (kə-**rekt**); whether it is an adjective or a verb, this word is pronounced with the second syllable stressed. Adding the prefix "in-" does not change the respective stress position, so "**incorrect**" is pronounced [ˌɪnkəˈrɛkt] (in-kə-**rekt**).

sequence [ˈsiːkwəns] (**seek**-wəns); it is easier to *seek* a number in a sequence than a number among some random heap of numbers.

subsequent [ˈsʌbsɪkwənt] (**sʌb**-sik-wənt); "subsequent" is something that comes next in a sequence, so you don't have to *seek* it any more; you know where it is. There is therefore no "seek" sound in "subsequent", and the stress is on the first syllable.

boar [bɔːˑ] (**baw**) UK, [bɔːr] (**baw'r**) US; a boar could bore a significant hole in your hand if you tried to pet one on a hiking trip. It's not how it got its name, but it is a way to remember it.

hockey [ˈhɒkʰi] (**hok**-ee) UK, [ˈhɑːki] (**haa**-kee) US; hockey matches are some of the *key* events in the US. Don't pronounce "hockey" it with "ei" at the end.

jockey [ˈdʒɒki] (**dzhok**-ee) UK, [ˈdʒɑːki] (**dzhaa**-kee) US; the same situation as in the word above; the "key" part is pronounced as "k*ee*" (a "jockey" is someone who rides a horse in a race).

shoulder [ˈʃəʊldə] (**shəu'l**-də) UK, [ˈʃoʊldər] (**shoh'l**-də) US; two hundred years ago, showing a shoulder as a woman could indeed be considered beyond the pale. It is not such a problem nowadays, so don't be afraid of saying "show" in the word "shoulder" (it is not "sha*aul*").

octave [ˈɒktɪv] (**okk**-tiv) UK, [ˈɑːktɪv] (**aak**-tiv) US; the musical interval is also the only English word in which "ave" at the and is pronounced as "iv".

novel [ˈnɒvᵉl] (**novv**-l) UK, [ˈnɑːvᵉl] (**naa**-vl) US; it doesn't matter whether you mean a book genre or the adjective meaning "new, unusual"; there is no "no" in the pronunciation.

schizophrenia [ˌskɪtsəˈfriːniə] (**skits**-ə-**free**-ni-ə); a German heart will skip a beat when seeing this word; not just because schizophrenia was originally described and researched by German scientists, but also because its pronunciation resembles to a certain degree the original German one. It is one of very few English words containing the "ts" sound where "t" and "s" are pronounced almost simultaneously.

shovel [ˈʃʌvᵉl] (**shʌ**-vl); using a shovel you **shove** [ʃʌv] (shʌv) (forcefully push) material, not "show" it.

launch [lɔːntʃ] (**law'ntch**); as in most English words, "au" here is pronounced as [ɔː] (aw). Don't confuse the word with **lunch** [lʌntʃ] (**lʌntch**); you can launch a **rocket** [ˈrɒkɪt] (**rokk**-it) UK, [ˈrɑːkɪt] (**raa**-kit) US and you can have a lunch with your friends, but hopefully not otherwise.

dairy [ˈdɛəri] (**de**-ə-ri) UK, [ˈdɛri] (**de**-ri) US; how *dare* you pronounce this word wrong? If you *dare* to pronounce it, keep the "i" silent.

laugh [lɑːf] (**laaf**) UK, [læf] (**læf**) US; the letter combination "augh" is usually pronounced [ɔː] (aw), as in "taught", "caught", "naught", but not here.

vary [ˈvɛri] (**ve**-ri), in the UK also [ˈvɛəri] (**ve**-ə-ri); when something changes, it **ve**-r*eez*, not ve-**rise**. The first part in "**variable**" is pronounced the same as "vary", i.e. it is **ve**-ri-ə-bl, not ve-**raay**-ə-bl.

surface [ˈsɜːfɪs] (**sə'ə**-fis) [ˈsɝːfɪs] (**sər**-fis); you can wipe your face using the surface of your towel, but you cannot rhyme it with it.

clothes [kləʊðz] (**kləuðz**) or [kləʊz] (**kləuz**) UK, [kloʊðz] (**kloh'ðz**) or [kləʊz] (**kloh'z**) US; if you want to pronounce the word very articulately, you can pronounce the "th" as [ð] and then add [z] to it, but many people say just the [z] at the end.

month [mʌnθ] (**mʌnth**); some words starting with "mon" are pronounced with [ʌ], some with [ɒ] (o) UK or [ɑː] (aa) US. This one is of the first type, "**monarch**" would be an example of the second type, pronounced [ˈmɒnək] (**monn**-ək) UK, [ˈmɑːnək] (**maa**-nrk) or [ˈmɑːnɑːrk] (**maa**-naark) US.

front [frʌnt] (**frʌnt**); is pronounced with [ʌ], i.e. "ron" in it **doesn't** sound like the name "Ron". The same is true for "confront" [kən ˈfrʌnt] (kən-**frʌnt**).

oven [ˈʌvᵉn] (**ʌ**-vn); if you forget that you are baking something in an oven, you will probably say "oh" afterwards, but don't say it in the word itself.

stove [stəʊv] (**stəu'v**) UK, [stoʊv] (**stoh'v**) US; although a stove typically contains an oven underneath, there is no [ʌv] in its pronunciation.

exercise [ˈɛksəsaɪz] (**ek**-sə-saayz) UK, [ˈɛksəsaɪz] (**ek**-sr-saayz) US; many doctors will discourage you from eating too many eggs if you want to lead a healthy lifestyle. Whether they are right or not is a matter of discussion, but one thing is for sure: don't mix eggs and (the word) "exercise"; after all, it's "exercise" not "eggser-cise".

margarine [ˌmɑːdʒəˈriːn] (maa-dzhe-**reen**) UK, [ˈmɑːrdʒərɪn] (**maar**-dzhe-rin) US; in most dialects, the "g" is pronounced as [dʒ] (dzh) (perhaps it will help you to remember that margarine is also colloquially called "marge" [mɑːdʒ] (maadzh) in the UK). Also notice the difference in stress position between American and British English.

cupboard [ˈkʰʌbəd] (**kʌ**-bed) UK, [ˈkhʌbəd] (**kʌ**-brd) US is indeed derived from the words "cup" and "board"; nonetheless, the "board" in it is pronounced with [ə] and "p" is not pronounced at all.

company [ˈkʰʌmpəni] (**kʌm**-pe-nee); a company is a group of people who in a sense "come" together, and the "com" in "company" is pronounced exactly the same as in "come". The same is true for **accompany** [əˈkʰʌmpəni] (e-**kʌm**-pe-nee).

ability [əˈbɪləti] (e-**bil**-e-tee); although an ability is something you are **able** [ˈeɪbᵊl] (**ey**-bl) to do, there's no "ey" at the beginning of "ability".

village [ˈvɪlɪdʒ] (**vil**-idzh); it is not called so because its inhabitants are of higher age on average; in fact, there is no connection between the words "village" and "age" whatsoever, and there is also none in the pronunciation. The same applies to a **villager** [ˈvɪlɪdʒəʳ] (**vil**-idzh-e) UK, [ˈvɪlɪdʒɚ] (**vil**-idzh-rr) US.

mortgage [ˈmɔːɡɪdʒ] (**maw**-gidzh) UK, [ˈmɔːrɡɪdʒ] (**maw'r**-gidzh) US; the "t" is silent, as it should be in the name of Lord Voldemort according to J.K.Rowling (although most Muggles who dare say the name pronounce the final t). The "age" at the end has to do with how old people are approximately as much as in the case of "village".

island ['aɪlənd] (**aay**-lənd); written "iland" before the 16th century. Although island indeed is land surrounded by water, the word is not written so because it "is land", but because there is an etymologically unrelated word **isle** [aɪl] (pronounced the same as "I'll") which also means "island", and so people during the 16th century thought it would be fun to insert "s" into the spelling of "iland" as well.

aisle [aɪl] (**aayl**); a walkway along sections of seats, as in a **theatre** ['θɪətəʳ] (**thi-ə-tə**) UK, **theater** ['θiːətᵊ] (**thee-ə-tr**) US. It is pronounced exactly the same as "I'll" and "isle".

Finally, we will end this section by a few words that contain the group of letters "ough", which has 7 possible pronunciations. The easiest way to remember the correct one is to ignore some of the letters:

tough [tʌf] (**tʌf**) —something which is "tough" is "hard". Pronounced as "t_ough".

through [θruː] (**throo**); the word is pronounced as "thr_{ou}gh" and indeed, it is also sometimes written as "thru".

cough [kɒf] (**koff**) UK, [kɔːf] (**kaw'f**) US; pronounced as "c_{ou}gh".

thought [θɔːt] (**thaw't**); pronounced roughly as "th_{ough}t".

though [ðəʊ] (**ðəu**) UK, [ðoʊ] (**ðoh**) US; pronounced as "th_{ough}". A related word "**although**" is pronounced as "all th_{ough}", with stress on the second syllable.

bough [baʊ] (**baau**) is a literary word for a branch of a tree. It is pronounced as "**bou**gh".

thorough [ˈθʌrə] (**thʌ**-rə) UK, [ˈθɝːroʊ] (**thə**-rou) or [ˈθʌroʊ] (**thʌ**-roh) US; the American pronunciation can be remembered as "**thor**ough". "**Thoroughly**" is pronounced exactly the same (in the respective dialect), just with [li] (**lee**) at the end.

1.3 WORDS YOU SHOULD PROBABLY KNOW

The words in this section are not as common as the ones in the previous one, but once you reach a certain level of fluency in English, you will inevitably have to use them sooner or later, so it is advisable to learn them as well.

dessert [dɪˈzɜːt] (di-**zə'ət**), [dɪˈzɝːt] (di-**zərt**) is a sweet course that concludes the meal. Don't confuse it with **desert** [ˈdɛzət] (**de**-zət) UK, [ˈdɛzɚt] (**de**-zrt) US which is a large area of dry land.

veggie [ˈvɛdʒi] (**vedzh**-ee); in British English, you can "turn veggie", for example, which means that you become a **veg**etarian (the word "veggie" can refer to a vegetarian in general). In the US, the word is used mostly as an adjective meaning "**veg**etable". Anyway, in all these words, "veg" is pronounced with [dʒ] (dzh).

Arkansas [ˈɑːkənˌsɔː] (**aak**-ən-s*aw*) UK, [ˈɑːrkənˌsɔː] (**aark**-ən-s*aw*) US; the name of one of the US states sounds like a symbol for a new religious movement: "ark and saw". However, this is how it is really pronounced.

schedule [ˈʃɛdjuːl] (**shed**-yool) UK, [ˈskɛdʒuːl] (**skedzh**-ool) US; I am not sure which of the two variants is more confusing. Anyway, if you learn a certain dialect, you should stick to the pronunciation used in that dialect.

houses [ˈhaʊzɪz] (**haauziz**); the singular form, house, is pronounced with [s] at the end: [haʊs] (h*aa*us). The plural of it, however, is pronounced with [z].

sword [sɔːd] (**saw'd**) UK, [sɔːrd] (**saw'rd**) US; the "w" is silent, and the word is pronounced as if it were written "sord". However, it is not true that in "sw" the "w" would always be silent; for example "**swan**" is pronounced [swɒn] (**swonn**) UK, [swɑːn] (**swaan**) US.

thesaurus [θɪˈsɔːrəs] (thi-**saw**-rəs) is used by learners and native speakers alike to spice up their writing with better-looking words. Three things can go wrong with its pronunciation—the "the" at the beginning is [θɪ] (thi), not [ðə] (the), "au" in the second syllable is [ɔː] (aw), and the "s" that precedes it is [s], not [z].

despicable [dɪˈspɪkəbᵊl] (dis-**pik**-ə-bl), rarely also [ˈdɛspɪkəbᵊl] (**des**-pik-ə-bl); when you despise [dɪˈspaɪz] (dis-**paayz**) something, you find it "despicable", which is pronounced with [k] for some reason. The word "despisable" [dɪˈspaɪzəbᵊl] (dis-**paay**-zə-bl) (spelled with an "s") theoretically exists in some dictionaries, but no-one really uses it in practice.

maple [ˈmeɪpᵊl] (**mei**-pl); you can make a map (mæp) out of its wood, you can eat an apple (æ-pl) with its syrup, but don't pronounce it with [æ]. By the way, the word "**syrup**" is pronounced [ˈsɪrəp] (**si**-rəp), not "saay-rəp".

owl [aʊl] (**aaul**); it may be a silly way, but if you remember that an owl looks like ʌ(OO)ʌ, it will perhaps help you remember that it is pronounced with something close to "ʌoo".

owe [əʊ] (**əu**) UK, [oʊ] (**oh**) US; if you remember that the phrase "I owe you" is often abbreviated IOU, it will help you remember that this word is pronounced just as the letter "o". The abbreviation has even become a noun meaning "a written promise to pay a debt" (you can give someone "an IOU").

Ireland [ˈaɪələnd] (**aay**-ə-lənd) UK, [ˈaɪɚlənd] (**aay**-r-lənd) US; ironically, "ire", pronounced [ˈaɪəʳ] (**aay**-ə) UK, [ˈaɪɚ] (**aay**-r) US, is a word meaning "anger" or "wrath". However, the "Ire" in "Ireland" comes from "Ériu", a mythological Irish being.

ethics ['εθɪks] (**eth**-iks) is a set of moral principles. The word doesn't begin with the "ee" sound, and the same is true for **ethical** ['εθɪkᵊl] (**eth**-ik-l).

pupil ['pjuːpᵊl] (**pyoo**-pl) is a young student (schoolchildren under 18 are called pupils in the UK). Although a pupil is sort of a "human pup", this is not how the word was created. (A "pup" [pʌp] is a young of various animal species.)

determine [dɪˈtɜːmɪn] (di-**tə'ə**-min) UK, [dɪˈtɜːrmɪn] (di-**tər**-min) US; it wouldn't really make sense to try to "deter a mine" would it?

archangel ['ɑːkeɪndʒəl] (**aak**-eyn-dzhəl) UK, ['ɑːrkeɪndʒəl] (**ark**-eyn-dzhəl) US; in contrast to **arch** [ɑːtʃ] (**aatch**) UK, [ɑːrtʃ] (**artch**) US, this one is pronounced with a hard "ch". You can remember that the Mormon Church teaches that Noah (the builder of Noah's **Ark**) is actually the same person as Archangel Gabriel, if it helps you to remember the correct pronunciation.

archenemy ['ɑːtʃɛnəmi] (**aatch**-en-ə-mee) UK ['ɑrtʃɛnəmi] (**artch**-en-ə-mee) US; archenemy is the "opposite" of archangel, and thus differs in pronunciation as well.

agile ['ædʒaɪl] (**æ**-dzhaayl), in the US also ['ædʒᵊl] (**æ**-dzhl); don't pronounce this word as "ey-dzhl".

quantum ['kwɒntəm] (**kwon**-təm) UK, ['kwɑːntəm] (**kwaan**-təm) US; pay attention to the British pronunciation—the "a" is pronounced the same as "o" in "lot". Also, the "u" at the end is just [ə], not "oo".

gig [gɪg] (g'ig) is a common slang term for a musical performance. It looks as though it should be pronounced with "dzh" at the beginning, but it is not.

saliva [səˈlaɪvə] (sə-**laay**-və); if I *"say liver"*, will your mouth fill with saliva? For many people it won't, and the correct pronunciation is with a stress on the second syllable ("aliv" in it is pronounced as in "alive"), not with "say" at the beginning.

multiply [ˈmʌltɪplaɪ] (**mʌl**-tip-laay); just pay attention to the pronunciation of "u"; it is pronounced as in "but", not as in "put". The same is true for **multiple** [ˈmʌltɪpl] (**mʌl**-ti-pl).

vegetarian [ˌvɛdʒəˈtʰɛəriən] (vedzh-ə-**teə**-ri-ən) UK, [ˌvɛdʒəˈtɛriən] (vedzh-ə-**ter**-iən) US; "-tarian" at the end of a word is always pronounced as in "vegetarian", i.e. not "ey-ri-ən". The same is true for all "-arianism"s.

pescetarian [ˌpɛskəˈtɛəriən] (pes-kə-**teə**-ri-ən) UK, [ˌpɛskəˈtɛəriən] (*pes*-kə-**teə**-ri-ən) US; this neologism means "someone who eats fish but not land animals". Its pronunciation is somewhat confusing, because it is derived from Italian "pesce" which means "fish" but which is pronounced [ˈpeʃe] (**pe**-sheh) (in Italian).

vegan [ˈviːgən] (**vee**-gən); the city of **Las Vegas** [ˈlɑːs ˈveɪgəs] (**laas vei**-gəs) is considered to be a place of indulgence—a quality despised by vegans. Don't you dare pronounce the "veg" in the two words the same.

industry [ˈɪndəstri] (**in**-dəs-tree); unlike in **industrial** [ɪnˈdʌstriəl] (in-**dʌs**-tree-əl), the stress is on the first syllable, and the "u" is pronounced just as [ə].

competent [ˈkɒmpɪtənt] (**kom**-pit-ənt); "competent" and "compete" are derived from the same root, but the former is stressed on the first syllable while the latter on the second ("**compete**" is pronounced [kəmˈpiːt] (kom-**peet**)).

threshold [ˈθrɛʃhəʊld] (**thresh**-həuld), [ˈθrɛʃhoʊld] (**thresh**-hoh'ld); popular etymologies of the kind that "threshold" was a plank placed at the doorway to *hold* pieces of grains inside during *threshing* (getting rid of inedible parts of grains) are unfortunately completely wrong (the word comes from Old English " rescold"). Be it as it may, you can still use the popular etymology to remember that it is indeed pronounced as "thresh-hold".

analysis [əˈnæləsɪs] (ə-**nael**-ə-sis); although you analyse [ˈænəlaɪz] (**æn**-ə-l**aa**yz) something when you do an analysis, the two words are pronounced quite differently. The plural of "analysis" is "analyses" [əˈnæləsiːz] (ə-**nael**-ə-seez).

yogi [ˈjəʊgi] (**yəug**-ee) UK, [ˈjoʊgi] (**yoh'g**-ee) US; I don't think a yogi would be very happy if you called him "Yo, gee."

colonel [ˈkʰɜːnᵊl] (**kə'ə**-nl) UK, [ˈkʰɜːnᵊl] (**kər**-nl) US; is there a kernel inside a colonel (a military officer)? Well, at least in pronunciation, there is (they are pronounced the same).

heir [ɛə] (**eə**) UK, [ɛr] (**er**) US; a person who inherits something from someone else. It comes from Old French, so the "h" remains silent; it sounds exactly the same as "air" and "ere" (meaning "before long").

learned (person) [ˈlɜːnɪd] (**lə'ə**-nid) UK, [ˈlɜːrnɪd] (**lər**-nid) US; this pronunciation is used only when "learned" means "having a lot of knowledge" (e.g. a learned professor). "Learned" as the past tense of "learn" is pronounced [lɜːnd] (lə'ə-nd) UK, [lɜːnd] (lər'nd) US.

superfluous [suːˈpɜːfluəs] (soo-pə'ə-floo-əs) or [sjuːˈpɜːfluəs] (syoo-pə'ə-floo-əs) UK, [suːˈpɜːfluəs] (soo-**per**-floo-əs) US; you wouldn't want to catch a "superflu", would you? The word is stressed on the second syllable and the "u" in "fluous" is short.

era [ˈɪərə] (iə-rə) UK, [ˈɛrə] (er-ə) US; the correct pronunciation of this word is just a matter of dialect—if you learn British English, pronounce it with "iə" at the beginning, if you learn American English, pronounce it with "er" at the beginning (some Americans, however, pronounce it also [ˈɪrə] (ir-ə)).

compose [kəmˈpəʊz] (kəm-**pəuz**) UK, [kəmˈpoʊz] (kəm-**poh'z**) US; the stress in "compose" is on the second syllable, but in **composition** [ˌkɒmpəˈzɪʃ°n] (kom-pə-**zi**-shn) UK, [ˌkɑːmpəˈzɪʃ°n] (kaam-pə-**zi**-shn) US it is on the third one. "Decompose", on the other hand, is [ˌdiːkəmˈpəʊz] (dee-kəm-**pəuz**) UK, [ˌdiːkəmˈpoʊz] (dee-kəm-**poh'z**) US.

machete [məˈʃɛti] (mə-**shet**-ee); do farmers use a machete when they harvest tea? I don't know, but the two words rhyme.

dove [dʌv] (dʌv); the bird of the pigeon family is often used as a symbol of love, perhaps because the words are so similar. However, the word "dove" is becoming increasingly widespread as the past tense of "dive" (whose standard form is "dived"), and in this sense it is pronounced [dəʊv] (**dəuv**) UK, [doʊv] (**doh'v**) US.

utensil [juːˈtʰɛns°l] (yoo-**ten**-sl); once you know that the stress is on the second syllable, the pronunciation of this word becomes actually quite natural.

mechanism [ˈmɛkənɪzᵉm] (**mek**-ə-ni-zm) is stressed on the first syllable, but **mechanical** [məˈkænɪkᵉl] (mə-**kæ**-ni-kl) is stressed on the second syllable.

strategy [ˈstrætədʒi] (**stræ**-tə-dzhee); unlike in the word "strategic" [strəˈtiːdʒɪk] (strə-**tee**-dzhik), there is no "tea" in "strategy".

preference [ˈprɛfᵉrəns] (**pref**-ə-rəns); notice the difference between "preference" and the verb "prefer" [prɪˈfɜː] (pri-**fə'ə**) UK, [prɪˈfɜː] (pri-**fər**) US.

bruise [bruːz] (**brooz**); a blue mark appearing under skin after being hit. As in "fruit", the "i" is silent.

angina pectoris [ænˈdʒaɪnəˈpɛktərɪs] (æn-**dzhai**-nə **pek**-tə-ris) is a severe pain in the chest caused by partial blockage of arteries.

tortoise [ˈtɔːtəs] (**taw**-təs) UK, [ˈtɔːrtəs] (**taw'r**-təs) US; how exactly to use the words "tortoise" (as opposed to "turtle") in common speech is slightly more complicated (it depends on the dialect you speak), but biologically tortoises are just one particular family of turtles. Anyway, the "i" is silent.

court [kʰɔːt] (**kaw't**) [kʰɔːrt] (**kaw'rt**); hopefully you will never have to deal with a court, but if you do, remember to pronounce it with "aw", not with "oo".

hindsight [ˈhaɪndsaɪt] (**haaynd**-saayt); after something happens, you have a much better understanding ("in hindsight") of what would have been appropriate to do in such a situation, and this understanding is called "hindsight". The "hind" is etymologically related to "behind", and so is the pronunciation. On the other hand, "**hinder**" is also etymologically related to "behind", but is pronounced [ˈhɪndə] (**hin**-də) UK, [ˈhɪndɚ] (**hin**-dr) US, as well as **hindrance** [ˈhɪndrəns] (**hin**-drəns).

rationale [ˌræʃəˈnɑːl] (ræ-shə-**naal**) UK, [ˌræʃəˈnæl] (ræ-shə-**næl**) US means "reasons explaining a particular decision". The "ale" at the end is misleading. There are only three English words in which "ale" at the end is pronounce in this way; the other two are **morale** [məˈrɑːl] (mə-**raal**) UK, [məˈræl] (mə-**ræl**) US which means "the amount of confidence that a person or a group of people has" and **chorale** [kɒˈrɑːl] (kor-**aal**) UK, [kəˈræl] (kə-**ræl**) US (a piece of church music).

finale [fɪˈnɑːli] (fin-**aa**-lee) UK, [fɪˈnæli] (fin-**æ**-lee) US is the last part of a show or a piece of music. And the only English word in which "ale" at the end is pronounced with "lee".

gizmo [ˈgɪzməʊ] (**g'iz**-məu) UK, [ˈgɪzmoʊ] (**g'iz**-m*oh*) US; a nonsensical placeholder name for a device which you don't know the proper term for. Don't pronounce it with [dʒ] (dzh) at the beginning! Otherwise you could get a few funny looks as people would understand it as "jizm of" ("jizm" is a slang term for semen).

mischief [ˈmɪstʃɪf] (**mis**-tchif); mischief is a bad behaviour which does not cause serious harm. Don't pronounce it with "k". The adjective derived from it is **mischievous** [ˈmɪstʃɪvəs] (**mis**-tchiv-əs);

miscellaneous [ˌmɪsəˈleɪniəs] (mis-ə-**lei**-nee-əs); learners make miscellaneous mistakes; even the word "miscellaneous" is often one of them.

lozenge [ˈlɒzɪndʒ] (**lozz**-indzh) UK, [ˈlɑːzɪndʒ] (**laa**-zindzh) US; a diamond-like figure: ◊. The last "e" is silent and there is no "oh" in it.

chic [ʃiːkʰ] (**sheek**); what is chic is fashionable or elegant. The word is borrowed from French and retains the original pronunciation.

lingerie [ˈlænʒəri] (**læn**-zhə-ree) UK, [ˌlɑːn(d)ʒəˈreɪ] (laan-(d)zhə-**rei**) or [ˈlɑn(d)ʒəri] (**laan**-(d)zhə-ree) US; in British English, pronunciation of this word remains close to the original French one; there are several other options in American English.

coeliac (disease) [ˈsiːliːæk] (**see**-lee-æk, spelled "celiac" in the US); an autoimmune disease caused by reaction of the small intestine to gluten. Especially the British spelling can be somewhat misleading in terms of pronunciation.

prodigal [ˈprɒdɪgəl] (**prodd**-ig-əl) UK, [ˈprɑːdɪgᵉl] (**praad**-ig-əl) US; one has to be almost a **prodigy**, pronounced [ˈprɒdɪdʒi] (**prodd**-idzh-ee) UK or [ˈprɑːdɪdʒi] (**praad**-idzh-ee) US, in order to remember that "prodigal" is pronounced with [g] instead of [dʒ] (dzh).

Boolean [ˈbuːliən] (**boo**-lee-ən); every programmer knows this word, but many pronounce it (wrongly) with [liːn] (leen) at the end.

ado [əˈduː] (ə-**doo**); known mostly from the title of Shakespeare's play Much Ado About Nothing. It is easy to remember the correct pronunciation once you see that it is actually composed out of two words "a" and "do".

versatile [ˈvɜːsətaɪl] (**və'ə**-sə-taayl) UK, [ˈvɜːrsətaɪl] (**vər**-sə-taayl) or [ˈvɜːsətᵉl] (**vər**-sə-tl) US; the word means "being able to do many different things". The "tile" is usually pronounced as the actual "tile", but in some dialects also [tᵉl] (tl).

pasture [ˈpʰɑːstʃəʳ] (**paas**-tchə) UK, [ˈpʰæstʃɚ] US (**pæs**-tchr); think of pasture, a grassland for cattle, as about part of na**ture** being more common in the **past**.

paradigm [ˈpʰærədaɪm] (**pæ**-rə-daaym); the pronunciation is quite natural, but some people are 'digging' this word a little bit too much. There is no 'dig' sound inside it.

lieutenant [lɛfˈtʰɛnənt] UK (lef-**te**-nənt), [luːˈtʰɛnənt] US (loo-**te**-nənt); the American pronunciation poses no problem here; just notice the British one.

debris [ˈdɛbriː] (**deb**-ree) UK, [dəˈbriː] (də-**bree**) US; this word retained its original French pronunciation, so the final "s" is silent.

hyperbole [haɪˈpʰɜːbəli] (haay-**pə'ə**-bə-l*ee*) UK, [haɪˈpʰɝːbəli] US (haay-**pər**-bə-l*ee*); don't confuse this word with a hyperbola, a geometric shape. Hyperbole is a form of exaggeration, and it doesn't rhyme with a bowl.

antipodes [ænˈtʰɪpədiːz] (æn-**tip**-ə-deez); a word describing two points which are directly opposite to each other on a sphere. For some reason, it doesn't rhyme with an "**antipode**" [ˈæntɪˌpəʊd] (æn-tip-əu'd) UK, [ˈæntɪˌpoʊd] (æn-tip-*oh*'d) US, which is the singular form of it and which does rhyme with words like "mode" or "code".

epitome [ɪˈpʰɪtəmi] (ih-**pit**-ə-m*ee*); this somewhat less common word means "someone who is a prototypical example of a class of people". Although you could fill a tome with a list of epitomes, you cannot rhyme it with them.

vintage [ˈvɪntɪdʒ] (**vin**-tidzh); this word means primarily "the yield of wine from one particular year", but as an adjective, it started to be used for anything that is "like something old and high quality", e.g. "vintage guitars". Although it looks slightly like "vine age", there is no etymological connection between "vintage" and the words "age", and there is also none in the pronunciation (which is hardly an argument, because "vin" in "vintage" is in fact is related to "vine", and it is pronounced differently).

unanimous [juːˈnænɪməs] (yoo-**næ**-ni-məs); this word is not "unanimous" which could theoretically mean "not possessing animosity", but which unfortunately does not exist. Rather it comes from Latin ūnus (one) + animus (mind) and means "of one mind", "in agreement".

Brontë [ˈbrɒntʰiː] (**bron**-tee); as most English words that should theoretically end with the [ɛ] sound are in fact pronounced with [eɪ] (ey) at the end, such as "**soufflé**" [ˈsuːfleɪ] (**soo**-flei) UK, [suːˈfleɪ] (soo-**flei**) US or "**ballet**" [ˈbæleɪ] (**bæ**-lei) UK, [bælˈeɪ] (bæ-**lei**) US, some people tend to read names such as those of Charlotte, Emily, and Anne Brontë (famous British poets and novelists) with [eɪ] (ey) at the end. You can think about the two dots as about a hint that you should actually pronounce it as "**ee**".

ton [tʌn] (tʌn); don't let your mother tongue mislead you; there is really an [ʌ], and so is in "**son**" and "**won**". What may be even more confusing than the pronunciation is the fact that "ton" refers to the unit used in the US that is defined as 1 ton = 2,000 pounds = 907 kg. It can also refer to the ton used in the UK where 1 ton = 2,240 pounds = 1,016 kg, but which is no longer officially used (since 1985). If you want to refer to the so called "**metric ton**", the word you are looking for is pronounced the same but is spelled "tonne", i.e. 1 tonne = 1000 kg.

crow [krəʊ] (**krəu**) UK, [kroʊ] (**kroh**) US is a common name for a certain genus of birds from which some of the best know are ravens. It rhymes with "low", not with "cow".

mishap [ˈmɪshæp] (**mis-hæp**); the word is mis-hap, meaning mis-happiness, i.e. misfortune or bad luck.

survey [ˈsɜːveɪ] (**sə'ə-vei**) UK, [ˈsɜːveɪ] (**sər-vei**) US; some words ending with "ey" are pronounced with [i] (**ee**) at the end, such as **chimney** [ˈtʃɪmni] (**tchim-nee**) and **baloney** [bəˈləʊni] (**bə-ləu-nee**) UK, [bəˈloʊni] (**bə-loh-nee**) US, but "survey" is not one of them. "Baloney" is an informal word used especially in American English to mean "nonsense, rubbish".

valve [vælv] (**vælv**); the final "e" is silent, but it doesn't modify the first vowel to "ey".

granite [ˈɡrænɪt] (**græ-nit**); the "nite" at the end looks like as though it should be pronounced like "night", but it is not.

fuchsia [ˈfjuːʃə] (**fyoo-shə**) is a small bush with flowers of a characteristic colour which is also referred to as "fuchsia".

bellows [ˈbɛləʊz] (**bel-əuz**) UK, [ˈbɛloʊz] (**bel-oh'z**) US is an instrument used to blow air. Apart from the difference in pronunciation from the word "below" (which is not related to it), notice that "bellows" is a singular noun (i.e. we say "bellows is").

alibi [ˈælɪbaɪ] (**æl-ə-baay**); if you know any Romance language, you will be probably terrified by how this word is pronounced in English, but you will have to live with it.

oasis [əʊˈeɪsɪs] (**əu-ey-sis**) UK, [oʊˈeɪsɪs] (**oh-ey-sis**) US; imagine you are on a desert with a friend named Asis and you are almost dying of thirst. When you cannot go any further, you say "oh, Asis..." after which your friend starts running forward in a burst of happiness. To solve the puzzle, find out why. The plural of "oasis" is "oases" [əʊˈeɪsiːz] (əu-**ey**-seez) UK, [oʊˈeɪsiːz] (oh-**ey**-seez) US.

canoe [kʰəˈnuː] (kə-**noo**); notice the stress on the second syllable and the pronunciation of "oe".

zealot [ˈzɛlət] (**zel**-ət) is a person who is very enthusiastic about something, i.e. a person having a great amount of **zeal** (a great energy or enthusiasm) which is, surprisingly, pronounced [ziːl] (zeel).

miniature [ˈmɪnətʃəʳ] (**min**-ə-tchə) UK, [ˈmɪnətʃɚ] (**min**-ə-tchr) [ˈmɪnətʃʊr] (**min**-ə-tchoor) US; the "a" in the word "miniature" is sort of miniature—in fact, it isn't there at all (in pronunciation).

enveloped [ɪnˈvɛləpt] (in-**vel**-əpt), meaning "surrounded by something", this word is in fact the past participle of the verb "envelop" [ɪnˈveləp] (in-**vel**-əp). It is not derived from the noun **envelope** [ˈɛnvələʊp] (**en**-vəl-əup) UK, [ˈɛnvələʊp] (**en**-vəl-oh'p) US.

banal [bəˈnɑːl] (bə-**naal**); some Americans pronounce the word also as [ˈbeɪnᵉl] (bei-nl), but I would recommend sticking to the former pronunciation. Not only does it sound more educated; it also reduces the odds of an awkward situation if someone doesn't catch the "b" at the beginning.

cottage [ˈkɒtɪdʒ] (**kott**-idzh) UK, [ˈkɑːtɪdʒ] (**kaat**-idzh) US; some people think that this word (meaning "a small house in the country") comes from French, perhaps because of its similarity with **massage** [məˈsɑːʒ] (mə-**saazh**). Although there is a word "cottage" in French, it was borrowed from English to describe small houses in the English country.

1.4 WORDS THAT MIGHT BE USEFUL

This section contains words that you will most likely meet just in written form, but depending on your field of interest, they might be useful as well. You might want to skip to the second part of this book during the first reading and return to this section later.

albeit [ɔːlˈbiːɪt] (*aw'l*-bee-it) this fairly formal word, meaning "although", is not used much in speech, but is still quite common in literature. Once you remember that it is actually a combination of three words "all be it", you will no longer have any problem with its correct pronunciation.

caveat [ˈkʰævɪˌæt] (**kæv**-ee-æt) or [ˈkʰævɪˌɑːt] (**kæv**-ee-aat), in the UK also [ˈkʰævɛˌɑːt] (**kæ**-ve-aat); meaning "a warning", it is not so common in speech, but still appears in literature or official documents. Just remember that you can't eat a caveat. Especially not in a cave.

scythe [saɪð] (**saayð**); now, when the Death comes for you, you can try to compliment him by saying what a nice scythe he has. I cannot guarantee he will let you go, though.

Edinburgh [ˈɛdɪnbərə] (**ed**-in-bə-rə) or [ˈɛdɪnbrə] (**ed**-in-brə) UK, [ˈɛdənbʌrə] (**ed**-ən-bʌ-rə) or [ˈɛdənbərə] (**ed**-ən-bə-rə) US; the name of the capital of Scotland is known well enough to slip into many other languages in an almost unchanged written form, but its correct counter-intuitive pronunciation is usually known only to native speakers.

blessed (adjective) [ˈblɛsɪd] (**bles**-id); when "blessed" is the past tense or the past participle of "bless", it is pronounced as one would expect: [blɛst] (**blest**), but when it is an adjective, it is pronounced with "id" at the end, as in "a moment of blessed calm" or "blessed are the poor".

tapestry ['tæpəstri] (**tæp**-əs-tree); although rolled up tapestries resemble tapes, their pronunciation doesn't even *try*.

valet ['væleɪ] (**væ**-lei) or ['vælɪt] (**væ**-lit), in the US also [væˈleɪ] (**væ**-**lei**) is a personal servant. Not to be confused with "wallet" ['wɒlɪt] (**woll**-it) UK, ['wɑːlɪt] (**waa**-lit) or ['wɔːlɪt] (**w'aw**-lit) US which is the little thing in which we usually transport money.

eerie ['ɪəri] (**ih**-ə-ree) UK, ['ɪri] (**ih**-ree) US is an adjective meaning "strange and frightening".

psoriasis [səˈraɪəsɪs] (sə-**raay**-ə-sis) is a very inconvenient, incurable, and non-contagious skin disease.

centaur ['sɛntɔː'] (**sen**-taw) UK, ['sɛntɔːr] (**sen**-taw'r) US; half man, half horse—legends about this creature are many **cen**turies old. This will hopefully help you remember that the first letter is pronounced as "s", not as "k".

crescent ['krɛsᵉnt] (**kre**-snt) or ['krɛzᵉnt] (**kre**-znt); a figure looking like the first or the third quarter moon: ☽. It is also used as a symbol of Islam.

crescendo [krəˈʃɛndəʊ] (krə-**shen**-dəu) UK, [krəˈʃɛndoʊ] (krə-**shen**-doh) US; although both "crescent" and "crescendo" originate in Latin "crescere" (to grow), the latter one was borrowed to the English musical terminology from Italian and means "increasing in loudness". Its pronunciation is close to the Italian one.

covet ['kʰʌvət] (**kʌ**-vət); a verb meaning "to want something very much". It has nothing to do with a **cove** [kʰəʊv] (**kəuv**) UK, [kʰoʊv] (**koh'v**) US which means "a small bay".

covenant [ˈkʰʌvənənt] (**kʌv**-ə-nənt); covenant is a form of agreement or contract. Again, it has nothing to do with "cove".

papyrus [pʰəˈpʰaɪrəs] (pə-**paay**-rəs); the word comes from Latin, but the pronunciation is now completely an English one.

coup d'état [kʰuːdeɪˈtaː] (koo dey-**taa**); a coup (or coup d' tat) is a sudden, illegal, and often violent change of government. As is apparent both from its written and spoken form, it comes from French.

crustacean [kʰrʌˈsteɪʃən] (krʌ-**stey**-shn); little creatures living in the ocean. They are named so because of their crust [krʌst] and "cean" is pronounced exactly as in "o**cean**".

lineage [ˈlɪniːɪdʒ] (**lin**-ee-idzh); the line of descendants from an ancestor. It comes from Old French "linage" which originally comes from Latin "linea" (line). While the pronunciation of "i" in "line" had changed in English over time, the one in "lineage" had not.

algae in the UK usually [ˈælgiː] (**ælg**-ee), in the US usually [ˈældʒiː] (**æl**-dzhee); very simple plants growing in water. Notice the [iː] at the end and pay attention especially to the British pronunciation with hard "g".

hiatus [haɪˈeɪtəs] (haay-**ey**-təs) UK, [haɪˈeɪrəs] (haay-**ey**-dəs) US; it would be hard to get the pronunciation right just by guessing. The word means "a pause in activity when nothing happens".

Abelian [əˈbiliən] (ə-**bee**-lee-ən) or [əˈbiljən] (ə-**beel**-yən); just another word for "commutative" in mathematics, named in honour of Niels Henrik Abel [nils ˈhɛnrɪk ˈɑbəl] (nils **hen**-rik **aa**-bəl), not after **Abel** [ˈeɪbəl] (**ei**-bəl), the second son of Adam and Eve.

quay [kʰiː] (**kee**) UK, in the US also [kʰeɪ] (**kei**) or [kʰweɪ] (**kwei**); quay
is the part of a harbour where ships can dock; it is therefore one
of the "key parts" of a harbour.

forage [ˈfɒrɪdʒ] (**for**-idzh) UK, [ˈfɔːrɪdʒ] (**faw**-ridzh) or [ˈfɑːrɪdʒ] (**faa**-
ridzh) US; a noun meaning "food for horses or cattle" or a verb
meaning "to search for food". It seems to be composed from
"for" and "age", but it is not.

ligature [ˈlɪɡətʃəʳ] (**lig**-ə-tchə) UK, [ˈlɪɡətʃɚ] (**lig**-ə-tchr) US; in typo-
graphy, ligature means several glyphs connected to a single character; for example "ffi" in which twice "f" and once "i" are connected is some fonts. Although ffi looks a little like a gate, there is
no "gate" in the pronunciation.

ere [ɛə] (**eə**) UK, [ɛr] (**er**) US; this word is pronounced exactly the
same as "air" and "heir" and means "before". It is quite rare in
modern literature and is used mostly to create a poetic or archaic
feeling, but it is quite common in older literature.

Penelope [pʰəˈnɛləpʰi] (pə-**nel**-ə-pee); the wife of **Odysseus** [əʊ
ˈdɪsiəs] (əu-**dis**-ee-əs) or [əʊˈdɪsjus] (əu-**dis**-yoos) UK, in the US
with [ou] (*oh*) at the beginning, may have received many an envelope with an ode that she had legs slim like an antelope, but
she nevertheless remained faithful to her husband during his ab-
sence. Perhaps because the authors tried to rhyme **antelope**
[ˈæntɪləʊp] (**æn**-til-əup) UK, [ˈæntloup] (**ænt**-*loh*'p) US with her
name.

awry [əˈraɪ] (ə-**raay**)—this word shares a common root with "wry",
which means (among others) "abnormally bent or turned". Awry
means also "with a turn or twist to one side" or also "away from
the expected or proper direction" (for example in "Our plans
went awry").

Bayesian ['beɪzɪən] (**bei**-zi-ən); if you are a mathematician, like me, you may be pronouncing this word incorrectly, as I used to.

diaeresis [daɪˈɛrəsɪs] (daay-**er**-ə-sis) is the diacritical mark consisting of two dots above a letter (e.g. ë). In English; it is used only in a few borrowed words and proper names.

facade [fəˈsɑːd] (fə-**saad**); this word, meaning the front of a building, originates in French, and the pronunciation is still close to the French one.

archipelago [ˌɑːkʰɪˈpʰɛləgəʊ] (aa-ki-**pel**-ə-gəu) UK, [ˌɑːrkɪˈpʰɛləgoʊ] (aar-ki-**pel**-ə-goh) US is an island group.

purgatory [ˈpɜːgətri] (**pə'ə**-gə-tree) UK, [ˈpɜˌgəˌtɔːri] (**pr**-gə-taw-ree) US; the place (or rather a state of being) which, according to Catholic teachings, serves for purification from sins of those who are not ready to go directly to heaven. Due to a related word **purge** [pɜːdʒ] (**pə'ə-dzh**) UK, [pɜːdʒ] (**pərdzh**) US (to cleanse, to get rid of), people tend to mispronounce it with "dzh".

Yosemite [joʊˈsɛmɪtʰiː] (yəu-**sem**-it-ee) UK, [joʊˈsɛmɪriː] (yoh-**sem**-id-ee) US; Yosemite National Park is well known around the Globe. Although there certainly is at least one mite somewhere in the park, there is none in the name.

gynaecology [ˌgaɪnəˈkɒlədʒi] (gaay-nə-**koll**-ə-dzhee) UK, **gynecology** [ˌgaɪnəˈkɑːlədʒi] (gaay-nə-**kaa**-lə-dzhee) US; there are some people who pronounce "gynecology" with "dzh" at the beginning, perhaps because of words like **gyroscope** [ˈdʒaɪrəskəʊp] (**dzhaay**-rə-skəup) UK, [ˈdʒaɪrəskoʊp] (**dzhaay**-rə-skoh'p) US and **vagina** [vəˈdʒaɪnə] (və-**dzhaay**-nə). Nevertheless, the pronunciation with hard "g" at the beginning is much more common.

eschew [ɪsˈtʃuː] (iss-**tchoo**) means "to deliberately avoid something". If it helps you, you can imagine chewing food to avoid parts hard to swallow.

Ptolemy [ˈtɒləmi] (**toll**-ə-mee) UK, [ˈtɑːləmi] (**taa**-lə-mee) US; the famous Graeco-Roman mathematician and astronomer is pronounced without the "p" at the beginning and with "mee", not "my", at the end.

1.5 ALPHABETICAL INDEX OF PART I

PART II

COMMON ERROR
PATTERNS

II.1 INTERACTION WITH MOTHER TONGUE

We all have a mother tongue which functions as a filter for what sounds we are able to distinguish. When you learn a foreign language, you have to understand that it uses a different set of sounds and different orthographic rules than your mother tongue (i.e. the same letter or a letter group written in a different language may be pronounced differently).

What learners often do is that they read words as if they were written in their native language. Here are the most common errors of this type.

"au" *in English is* <u>*not*</u> *pronounced as "aoo"*; it is almost always pronounced as [ɔː] (*aw*, as in "saw"); for example "auto-" is pronounced [ɔːtə] (*aw-tə*), as in **autobiography** [ˌɔːtəbaɪˈɒɡrəfi] (*aw-tə-baay-**ogg**-rə-fee*) UK, [ˌɔːtəbaɪˈɑːɡrəfi] (*aw-tə-baay-**aag**-rə-fee*) US and **autopsy** [ˈɔːtɒpsi] (*aw-top-see*) UK, [ˈɔːrɑpsi] (*aw-dap-see*) US.

"ps" *at the beginning of a word is* <u>*not*</u> *pronounced "p+s"*; it is pronounced just as [s], such as in **psychology** [saɪˈkɒlədʒi] (*saay-**koll**-ə-dzhee*) UK, [saɪˈkɑːlədʒi] (*saay-**kaa**-lə-dzhee*) US or **pseudonym** [ˈsuːdənɪm] (**soo**-də-nim), in the UK also [ˈsjuːdənɪm] (**syoo**-də-nim).

"eu" *is* <u>*not*</u> *pronounced "eoo"*; unlike perhaps in all other languages, in English, it is pronounced [juː] (*yoo*, mostly UK) or [uː] (*oo*, mostly US), and sometimes also short ([jʊ] or [ʊ]). Examples include **Euclid** [juːˈklɪd] (*yoo-klid*), **pneumatic** [njuːˈmætɪk] (*nyoo-**mæt**-ik*) UK, [njuːˈmærɪk] (*noo-**mæ**-dik*) US, or **neuron** [ˈnjʊərɒn] (**nyoo**-ə-ron) UK , [ˈnʊrɑːn] (**noo**-raan) US.

"pn" *at the beginning of a word is* <u>*not*</u> *pronounced as "p+n"*; it is pronounced just as [n], e.g. **pneumatic** [njuːˈmætɪk] (*nyoo-**mæt**-ik*) UK, [njuːˈmærɪk] (*noo-**mæ**-dik*) US, **pneumonia** [njuːˈməʊniə] (*nyoo-**məu**-nee-ə*) UK, [nuːˈmoʊniə] (*noo-**moh**-nee-ə*) US.

"kn" *at the beginning of a word is* <u>not</u> *pronounced as "k+n"; it is pro-*nounced just as [n], e.g. **know** [nəʊ] (**nəu**) UK, [noʊ] (**noh**) US, **knee** [niː] (**nee**), **knife** [naɪf] (**naayf**).

"gn" *at the beginning of a word is* <u>not</u> *pronounced as "g+n"; it is,* as in the previous two cases, pronounced as [n], such as in **gnome** [nəʊm] (**nəum**) UK, [noʊm] (**noh'm**) US, and **gnash** [næʃ] (**næsh**). The word **gnocchi** can be pronounced according to this rule as [ˈnɒki] (**nokk**-*ee*) UK, [ˈnjɑːki] (**nyaa**-*kee*) US, but it is more common to pronounce it as [ˈɲɒki] (**ñokk**-*ee*) UK, [ˈɲɑːki] (**ñaa**-*kee*) US, where "ñ" represents a soft n, as in Spanish (gn in French or Italian).

"x" *at the beginning of a word is* <u>not</u> *pronounced as "ks"; it is pro-*nounced as [z], for example **xenophobia** [ˌzɛnəˈfəʊbiə] (zen-ə-**fəu**-*bee*-ə) UK, [ˌzɛnəˈfoʊbiə] (zen-ə-**foh**-*bee*-ə) US (one of several possible pronunciations) or **Xena** [ˈziːnə] (**zee**-nə), a fictional character.

"w" *is* <u>never</u> *pronounced as "v"; many languages don't have the "w"* sound (such as in the word "wow"), and the learners stubbornly pronounce English w as v (as in "very"). However, the distinction is sometimes crucial to be understood, such as in the words "vest" (a piece of garment) and "west" (one of the cardinal directions), or "vary" ("to be changing") and "wary" (meaning "careful"). To say "w", you have to make a narrow "slit" with your mouth with lips not touching the teeth.

"v" *is* <u>never</u> *pronounced as "w"; those who do realize that English has* a sound as in "wow" often use this sound for all English words containing anything vaguely similar to it. However, the letter "v" is never pronounced as in "wow", but always as in "very", by making the lower lip touching upper teeth.

"ch" *is not pronounced as "ch" (as in other languages);* the pronunciation rules for the digraph "ch" differ in all other languages from the English ones. In French it is [ʃ], which can still be heard in the English word **chef** [ʃɛf] (**shef**) (we will see more such words later), in German it can be [x] ("kh"), as in Scottish **Loch Ness** [ˌlɒxˈnɛs] (lokh **ness**). In standard English, however, it is virtually always either [tʃ] (chat, chalk, chapter) or [k] (character, chrome, orchestra), but there's no reliable rule to decide which one is the correct one, so it has to be remembered. Note: In some British dialects, the pronunciation is sometimes somewhere between [tʃ] and [ʃ].

"e" *is not always pronounced as in "get"*; "e" in non-stressed syllables is often pronounced as [ɪ] (as "i" in "hit"), especially in words beginning with "de-", "pre-", such as **detective** [dɪˈtɛktɪv] (di-**tek**-tiv), **pretend** [prɪˈtɛnd] (pri-**tend**). However, when "de-" is stressed, it is usually pronounced [dɛ] (de), e.g. **decorate** [ˈdɛkəˌreɪt] (**dek**-ə-reyt), but sometimes also [iː] (ee), e.g. "decrease" [ˈdiːkriːs] (**dee**-krees) when it is a noun (i.e. "a decrease").

"th" *in English is not pronounced as "s" or "dz"*; it is pronounced as [θ] (th) or [ð]; the former is pronounced similar to [t] and the latter similar to [d], but your tongue must touch the back side of your upper teeth, not just the upper palate. The distinction can be crucial—there was a funny German commercial for a language school, in which a young worker at the German Coast Guard receives a distress call: "Mayday, mayday Can you hear us We are sinking!", to which he replies, with a strong German accent: "Hallo What are you sinking about?"

"c" *is never pronounced as "ts" or "th"*; in some languages, "c" is pronounced as "ts" or "th" [θ], but in English, when it doesn't form a part of a larger letter group, it is almost always pronounced either as [s] before "e", "i" or "y" (e.g. cell, city, cyan) or as [kʰ] before "a", "o", and "u" (e.g. cap, cotton, cup) (or [k] in non-stressed syllables in some dialects).

"a" *is not pronounced as [ɛ] (e) (unless it follows "r", as in "care");* the letter "a" is usually pronounced "ey" (e.g. "lake") or "æ" (e.g. "cat"). The latter is often problematic for many learners, because it is halfway between "a" in "father" and "e" in "bed". A lot of learners don't notice the difference and pronounce it always as one of these, usually as "e", but none of the words "bet", "bat", and "but" sounds the same as any of the others.

"wr" *is not pronounced with "w" at the beginning;* there's no need to squeeze your lips while saying "wr"; it is pronounced just as "r". For example "write" and "rite" (and "wright" and "right") are all pronounced the same.

"r" *at the end of a word is not always silent in British English;* people learning British English often get an impression that "er", "or" etc. at the end of a word is pronounced just as [ə] (for example in "minister" ['mɪnɪstəʳ] (**min**-ist-ə). The [ʳ] in IPA (which is often denoted also by [(r)] in dictionaries) means that when such a word is pronounced without any context or is followed by a word that begins with a consonant, the "r" is silent, for example "minister sees" would be pronounced ['mɪnɪstə'siːz] (**min**-ist-ə **seez**), but when it's followed by a vowel, it is pronounced as [r], so "minister is" would be ['mɪnɪstə'rɪz] (**min**-ist-ə **riz**) (the "r" tends to be pronounced at the beginning of the following word).

II.2 O PRONOUNCED AS IN COME

Another common problem is the pronunciation of the letter "o". It is usually pronounced as [əʊ] UK or [oʊ] US, e.g. go, vote, hope, and [ɒ] UK or [ɑː] US, e.g. hot, god, pot.

There is, however, also another, less common pronunciation of "o", namely [ʌ]. For example, the word "come" is pronounced [kʰʌm]; the [ʌ] is the same sound as in "but" [bʌt]. Below is a list of the most common ones; I believe that if you are not a native speaker, some of them will surprise you. The underlined ones are especially commonly pronounced wrong.

among [əˈmʌŋ] (ə-m**ʌ**ng)

another [əˈnʌðəʳ] (ə-n**ʌ**-ðə) UK, [əˈnʌðɚ] (ə-n**ʌ**-ðr) US

brother [ˈbrʌðəʳ] (br**ʌ**-ðə) UK, [ˈbrʌðɚ] (br**ʌ**-ðr) US

colour [ˈkʰʌləʳ] (k**ʌ**-lə) UK, color [ˈkʰʌlɚ] (k**ʌ**-lr) US

come [kʰʌm] (k**ʌ**m)

comfortable [ˈkʰʌmfətəbᵉl] (k**ʌ**m-fə-tə-bl)

company [ˈkʰʌmpəni] (k**ʌ**m-pə-n*ee*)

cover [ˈkʰʌvəʳ] (k**ʌ**-və) UK, [ˈkʰʌvɚ] (k**ʌ**-vr) US

done [dʌn] (d**ʌ**n)

dove (a bird) [dʌv] (d**ʌ**v)

dozen [ˈdʌzᵉn] (d**ʌ**-zn)

front [frʌnt] (fr**ʌ**nt)

glove [glʌv] (gl**ʌ**v)

govern [ˈgʌvᵉn] (g**ʌ**-vn) UK, [ˈgʌvɚn] (g**ʌ**-vrn) US

honey [ˈhʌni] (h**ʌ**-n*ee*)

London [lʌndᵉn] (l**ʌ**n-dən)

love [lʌv] (l**ʌ**v)

Monday [ˈmʌndeɪ] (m**ʌ**n-dei)

money [ˈmʌni] (m**ʌ**-n*ee*)

monk [mʌŋk] (**mʌnk**)

monkey [ˈmʌŋki] (**mʌn**-k*ee*)

month [mʌnθ] (**mʌnth**)

mother [ˈmʌðəʳ] (**mʌ**-ðə) UK, [ˈmʌðɚ] (**mʌ**-ðr) US

none [nʌn] (**nʌn**)

nothing [ˈnʌθɪŋ] (**nʌ**-thing)

onion [ˈʌnjən] (**ʌn**-yən)

other [ˈʌðəʳ] (**ʌ**-ðə) UK, [ˈʌðɚ] (**ʌ**-ðr)

oven [ˈʌvᵉn] (**ʌ**-vn)

shove (to push forcefully) [ʃʌv] (**shʌv**)

shovel [ˈʃʌvl] (**shʌ**-vl)

some [sʌm] (**sʌm**)

son [sʌn] (**sʌn**)

stomach [ˈstʌmək] (**stʌ**-mək)

ton [tʌn] (**tʌn**)

tongue [tʌŋ] (**tʌng**)

won [wʌn] (**wʌn**)

wonder [ˈwʌndəʳ] (**wʌn**-də) UK, [ˈwʌndɚ] (**wʌn**-dr) US

II.3 Ch pronounced as sh

There are quite a few English words in which "ch" is pronounced as "sh" (mostly of French origin). The list below is ordered so that the most common words are listed first. Some of the words are not so well know, and so there is a short description of every single one. There is also a list of common proper names at the very end.

machine [məˈʃiːn] (**mə**-sheen) is piece of equipment with movable parts.

mustache [məˈstɑːʃ] (**mə**-**staash**) UK, [ˈmʌstæʃ] (**mʌ**-stæsh) or [məˈstæʃ] (**mə**-**stæsh**) US is a type of facial hair growing between the mouth and the nose.

chef [ʃɛf] (**shef**) is a professional senior cook.

chic [ʃiːk] (**sheek**) means "fashionable and elegant".

brochure [ˈbrəʊʃə] (**brəu**-shə) UK, [broʊˈʃʊr] (broh-**shoor**) US is a small booklet usually containing some condensed information, often of commercial type.

cache [kʰæʃ] (**kæsh**, the same as "cash") is used mostly in connection with computers where it means temporary data stored in such a way that they are can be accessed fast.

cliché [ˈkliːʃeɪ] (**klee**-shei) UK, [kliːˈʃeɪ] (klee-**shei**) US is a phrase that has been repeated for so long that people no longer find it interesting.

champagne [ʃæmˈpeɪn] (shæm-**peyn**) is a French sparkling white wine.

pistachio [pɪˈstæʃɪəʊ] (pis-**tæ**-shi-əu) or [pɪˈstɑːʃɪəʊ] (pis-**taa**-shi-əu)
UK, in the US with [oʊ] (*oh*) at the end, is a species of tree well
known for its nuts (which are also referred to as "pistachio").

parachute [ˈpærəʃuːt] (**pær**-ə-shoot) is a piece of cloth used to slow
down falling objects in the atmosphere.

fuchsia [ˈfjuːʃə] (**fyoo**-shə) is a small bush with flowers of a characteristic colour (a sort of dark pink) which is also referred to as
"fuchsia".

machete [məˈʃɛti] (mə-**shet**-ee) a large heavy knife used as a tool to
cut vegetation.

niche [niːʃ] (**neesh**) or [nɪtʃ] (**nitch**) originally referred to a cavity in a
wall used to place a bust or a statue. It is often used nowadays to
mean a "niche market", i.e. a certain specific market segment.

chauffeur [ʃɒˈfɜː] (shof-**fə'ə**) or [ˈʃəʊfə] (**sheu**-fə) UK, [ʃoʊˈfɜːr] (shoh-
fer) US is a personal car driver, usually of someone rich or important.

attaché [əˈtæʃeɪ] (ə-**tæ**-shei) UK, [ˌætəˈʃeɪ] (æ-tə-**shei**) US is a person
who works at an embassy, usually with a special responsibility.

chauvinist [ˈʃəʊvɪnɪst] (**shəu**-vin-ist) UK, [ˈʃoʊvɪnɪst] (**shoh**-vin-ist) US
originally meant a person who was unreasonably and aggress-
ively patriotic. In modern English, however, it is used mostly in
connection with male chauvinism—a chauvinist is then a man
who believes that men are superior to women.

charlatan [ˈʃɑːlətən] (**shaa**-lə-tən) UK, [ˈʃɑːrlətən] (**shaar**-lə-tən) US is
a person who claims to have knowledge or skills that he or she
does not really have.

echelon [ˈɛʃələn] (**esh**-ə-lonn) UK, [ˈɛʃəlɑːn] (**esh**-ə-laan) US is a level of authority.

chandelier [ˌʃændəˈlɪə] (shæn-də-**li**-ə) UK, [ˌʃændəˈlɪr] (shæn-də-**lir**) US is a round frame with branches holding lights or candles.

charade [ʃəˈrɑːd] (shə-**raad**) UK, [ʃəˈreɪd] (shə-**reyd**) US is a situation in which people pretend that something is true when it clearly is not.

ricochet [ˈrɪkəʃeɪ] (**rik**-ə-shei), in the UK also [ˈrɪkəʃɛt] (**rik**-ə-shet) is a verb meaning "to hit a surface and come off it fast at a different angle". When pronounced with [eɪ] at the end, the same pronunciation persists also in the derived terms "ricocheted" [ˈrɪkəʃeɪd] (**rik**-ə-sheyd) and "ricocheting" [ˈrɪkəʃeɪɪŋ] (**rik**-ə-shei-ing).

chateau [ˈʃætəʊ] (**shæ**-təu) UK, [ʃæˈtoʊ] (shæ-**toh**) US is a castle or a large country house in France. The plural is "chateaux", pronounced [ˈʃætəʊz] (**shæ**-təuz) UK, [ʃæˈtoʊz] (shæ-**toh'z**) US.

douche [duːʃ] (**doosh**) is a method of washing the inside of a woman's vagina using a stream of water. A douche bag is a device with a bag to be filled with fluid used for the cleaning process. A "douchebag" is a modern slang term meaning "an arrogant and rude person".

chivalry [ˈʃɪvəlri] (**shi**-vəl-ree) is a polite behaviour that shows a sense of honour, especially by men towards women.

chute [ʃuːt] (**shoot**) is a tube through which people or things can slide (such as in a water park).

chassis [ˈʃæsi] (**shæ**-see) is an inside frame of a vehicle.

chemise [ʃəˈmiːz] (shə-**meez**) is a piece of women's underwear or a nightdress.

quiche [kiːʃ] (**keesh**) is a certain type of pie.

chaise [ʃeɪz] (**sheyz**) is a carriage pulled by a horse.

chiffon [ˈʃɪfɒn] (**shi**-fon) UK, [ʃɪˈfɑːn] (shi-**faan**) US is a type of fine cloth.

pastiche [pæˈstiːʃ] (pæ-**steesh**) is a work of art that is created by deliberately copying the style of someone else

chanterelle [ˈʃɑːntərɛl] (**shaan**-tə-rel) or [ˌʃɑːntəˈrɛl] (shaan-tə-**rel**) is a common edible yellowish species of mushroom.

penchant [ˈpõʃõ] (**ponn**-shonn, with a nasal vowel) UK, [ˈpɛntʃənt] (**pen**-tchənt) US is a special liking for something, for example you can have a penchant for wine.

panache [pəˈnæʃ] (pə-**næsh**) or [pæˈnæʃ] (pæ-**næsh**), in the US also [pəˈnɑːʃ] (pə-**naash**) or [pæˈnɑːʃ] (pæ-**naash**) is an ornamental plume on a helmet.

chalet [ˈʃæleɪ] (**shæ**-lei) UK, [ʃæˈleɪ] (shæ-**lei**) US is a certain type of wooden house usually built in mountain areas.

cachet [ˈkæʃeɪ] (**kæ**-shei) UK, [kæˈʃeɪ] (kæ-**shei**) US; to have cachet means to have a quality other admire; for example a restaurant can lose its cachet if a good chef leaves it.

chagrin [ˈʃægrɪn] (**shæg**-rin)] UK, [ʃəˈgrɪn] (shə-**grin**) US is usually used in the phrase "to someone's chagrin" meaning "to one's disappointment"; for example "to his chagrin, neither of his projects were successful".

chaperone [ˈʃæpərəʊn] (**shæp**-ə-raun) UK, [ˈʃæpəroʊn] (**shæp**-ə-rohˈn) US is person who accompanies younger people (usually women) to ensure that they behave properly.

ruche [ruːʃ] (**roosh**) is a decorative fold on clothing or furniture.

crochet [ˈkrəʊʃeɪ] (**krəu**-shei) UK, [kroʊˈʃeɪ] (kroh-**shei**) US is a specific way of making clothes using a special thick needle.

louche [luːʃ] (**loosh**) is an adjective meaning "of questionable taste or morality", but often in an attractive way (for example "the louche world of the theater").

chenille [ʃəˈniːl] (shə-**neel**) is a type of cloth.

gauche [ɡəʊʃ] (**gəush**) UK, [ɡoʊʃ] (**goh'sh**) US is an adjective meaning "awkward or lacking social abilities".

COMMON PROPER NAMES

Charlotte [ˈʃɑːlət] (**shaa**-lət) UK, [ˈʃɑːrlət] (**shaar**-lət) US is a female given name. It is also the name of the largest city of the US state of North Carolina.

Michelle [mɪˈʃɛl] (mi-**shel**) is a female given name.

Chevrolet [ʃɛvrəˈleɪ] (shev-rə-**lei**) is a car brand.

Chicago [ʃɪˈkɑːɡoʊ] (shi-**kaa**-goh) or [ʃɪˈkɔːɡoʊ] (shi-**kaw**-goh) is a city in the US state of Illinois [ɪlɪˈnɔɪ] (ih-li-**noy**).

Michigan [ˈmɪʃɪgən] (**mi**-shi-gn) is one the US states.

Seychelles [seɪˈʃɛlz] (sei-**shelz**) is an island country near Madagascar.

Vichy [ˈvɪʃi] (**vish**-*ee*) is a brand of mineral water, a brand of cosmetics, and a town in France.

II.4 Common prefixes and postfixes

There are a few English prefixes and suffixes that are an especially common source of pronunciation errors, mostly because they would be pronounced differently if their position in a word were different. Some of the most common are listed in this section.

Postfixes

-ful *is pronounced [fl]*; for example **awful** [ˈɔːfᵊl] (*aw*-fl), **skilful** [ˈskɪlfᵊl] (**skil**-fl). The suffix "-ful" is often pronounced by foreigners the same as "full" (rhyming with "bull") and also often written with double "l", but neither such a spelling nor the pronunciation is correct.

-able *is pronounced [əbl]*; for example **noticeable** [ˈnəʊtɪsəbl] (**nəu**-tis-ə-bl), **doable** [ˈduːəbl] (**doo**-ə-bl). Learners of English often mispronounce it as "able" [ˈeɪbl] (**ey**-bl).

-age *is pronounced [ɪdʒ] (idzh)*; for example **village** [ˈvɪlɪdʒ] (**vil**-idzh), **mortgage** [ˈmɔːgɪdʒ] (**maw**-gidzh) UK, [ˈmɔːrgɪdʒ] (**maw'r**-gidzh) US.

-land *is pronounced as [lənd] in all names of countries*; for example England, Finland, Holland, Iceland etc. Other nouns of the form "somethingland" are usually pronounced as "something land", for example **grassland** [ˈgrɑːslænd] (**graas**-lænd) UK, [ˈgræslænd] (**græs**-lænd) US, and similarly marshland, swampland, dreamland, wonderland etc. The only four exceptions I am aware of in which "land" is pronounced the same as in the names of countries (i.e. [lənd]) are highland, lowland, dryland, and moorland.

-ical *is pronounced [ɪkl] (ikl)*; this itself causes little trouble, but the problem is that once you add the suffix "-ical" to a word, the stress moves to the last syllable before "-ical" (i.e. to the third syllable from the end). For example, **economy** is pronounced [ɪ ˈkɒnəmi] (ih-**kon**-ə-mee) UK, [ɪˈkɑːnəmi] (ih-**kaa**-nə-mee) US, whereas **economical** is pronounced [ˌiːkəˈnɒmɪkl] (ee-kə-**nom**-ikl) UK, [ˌiːkəˈnɑːmɪkl] (ee-kə-**naam**-ikl) US (both sometimes with [ˌɛkə] (ek-ə) at the beginning); **technology** is pronounced [tɛkˈnɒlədʒi] (tek-**noll**-ə-dzhee) UK, [tɛkˈnɑːlədʒi] (tek-**naa**-lə-dzhee) US, but **technological** is pronounced [ˌtɛknəˈlɒdʒɪkl] (tek-nə-**lodzh**-ikl) UK, [ˌtɛknəˈlɑːdʒɪkl] (tek-nə-**laadzh**-ikl) US.

PREFIXES

auto- *is pronounced* [ˌɔːtə] *(aw-tə)*; for example **autobiography** [ˌɔːtəbaɪˈɒɡrəfi] *(aw-tə-baay-**ogg**-rə-fee)* UK, [ˌɔːtəbaɪˈɑːɡrəfi] *(aw-tə-baay-**aag**-rə-fee)* US. The letter combination "au" is pronounced as [ɔː] *(aw)* in general.

de-, *when it is a prefix, is pronounced* [dɪ] *(di)* or [diː] *(dee)*; for example **decrease** [dɪˈkriːs] (di-**krees**) resp. [ˈdiːkriːs] (**dee**-krees) depending on whether it is a verb or a noun.

re-, *when it is a prefix, is pronounced as* [rɛ] *(re)*, [riː] *(ree)*, or [rɪ] *(ri)*; for example "**record**" in "to record something" (i.e. when it is a verb) is pronounced [rɪˈkɔːd] (ri-**kaw'd**) UK, [rɪˈkɔːrd] (ri-**kaw'rd**) US, but in "a record" (i.e. when it is a noun), it is pronounced [ˈrɛkɔːd] (**re**-kaw'd) UK, [ˈrɛkəd] (**rek**-rd) US.

in-, **im-**, **un-** *are pronounced* [ɪn] *(in)*, [ɪm] *(im)*, [ʌn] *and are usually not stressed (they sometimes carry a secondary stress)*; The important property to remember is that they don't influence the stress position in the word they modify; for example **incorrect** [ˌɪnkəˈrɛkt] (in-kə-**rekt**), **impossible** [ɪmˈpɒsɪbəl] (im-**pos**-ibl) UK, [ɪmˈpɑːsɪbəl] (im-**paas**-ibl) US, **unnecessary** [ʌnˈnesəsəri] (ʌn-**nes**-ə-sə-ree).

micro- is pronounced [maɪkrəʊ] (maay-krəu) UK, [ˌmaɪkroʊ] (maay-kroh) US; for example **microbiology** [ˌmaɪkrəʊbaɪˈɒlədʒi] (maay-krəu-baay-**oll**-ə-dzhee) UK, [ˌmaɪkroʊbaɪˈɑːlədʒi] (maay-kroh-baay-**aal**-ə-dzhee) US, **microgram** [ˈmaɪkrəʊɡræm] (**maay**-krəu-græm) UK, [ˈmaɪkroʊɡræm] (**maay**-kroh-græm) US. Notice, however, that **microscope** is pronounced [ˈmaɪkrəskəʊp] (**maay**-krə-skəu'p) UK, [ˈmaɪkrəskoʊp] (**maay**-krə-skoh'p) US, with "krə" instead of "krəu".

pre- as a prefix is not stressed and is pronounced [prɪ] (pri) or [priː] (pree); for example **pretend** [prɪˈtɛnd] (pri-**tend**), **presuppose** [ˌpriːsəˈpəʊz] (pree-sə-**pəuz**) UK, [ˌpriːsəˈpoʊz] (pree-sə-**poh'z**) US.

pro-, if it's not stressed, it is pronounced [prə]; for example **proliferate** [prəˈlɪfəreɪt] (prə-**liff**-ə-reyt), **propose** [prəˈpəʊz] (prə-**pəuz**) UK, [prəˈpoʊz] (prə-**poh'z**) US. When it is stressed, it is pronounced [prɒ] (pro, but not "prəu") in British English and [prɑː] (praa) in American English; for example **prosecute** [ˈprɒsɪkjuːt] (**pross**-ik-yoot) UK, [ˈprɑːsɪkjuːt] (**praa**-sik-yoot) US, **problem** [ˈprɒbləm] (**probb**-ləm) UK, [ˈprɑːbləm] (**praa**-bləm) US.

tri- meaning "three" is pronounced [traɪ] (**traay**); for example **tricycle** [ˈtraɪsɪkl] (**traay**-si-kl), **tripod** [ˈtraɪpɒd] (**traay**-pod) UK, [ˈtraɪpɑːd] (**traay**-paad) US.

II.5 HETERONYMS

There are many English words that are spelled the same but pronounced differently. Such words are called *heteronyms* (more loosely also *homographs*, but homographs can also be pronounced the same; they just mean different things). The widest class of heteronyms are words that change their meaning depending on where the stress is placed (this is the topic of the next section), but there are a few that are not of that kind. Here you can find a list of almost all of them.

read

(VERB) [riːd] (**reed**) means to perceive information provided in a written form.

(ADJ./VERB) [rɛd] (**red**) is the past tense of the verb "read".

live

(VERB) [lɪv] (**liv**) means "to be alive".

(ADJ) [laɪv] (**laayv**) is an adjective meaning "being alive".

wind

(NOUN) [wɪnd] (**win'd**) is a movement of air (it can also be a verb meaning "to blow to a wind instrument").

(VERB) [waɪnd] (**waaynd**) means "to turn, especially something around something else". For example, a river or a way can "waaynd", or you can "waaynd" a wire around a coil.

wound

(NOUN) [wuːnd] (**woond**) is an injury.

(ADJ/VERB) [waʊnd] (**waaund**) is the past tense of the verb "wind" (waaynd), see above.

tear

(VERB) [tʰɛəʳ] (**teə**) UK, [tʰɛr] (**ter**) US means "to rip a solid material" (it can also be a noun meaning a hole caused by tearing ['tʰɛrɪŋ] (**ter-ing**)).

(NOUN) [tʰɪəʳ] (**ti'ə**) UK, [tʰɪr] (**tir**) US is a water drop coming out of someone's eye.

bow

(NOUN) [bəʊ] (**bəu**) UK, [boʊ] (**boh**) US is a medieval weapon or a device used to play the violin and other bowed [bəʊd] (bəud) UK, [boʊd] (boh'd) US instruments (it can also be a verb meaning "to become bent" or "to play a bowed instrument").

(VERB) [baʊ] (baau) means "to bend yourself to show respect".

row

(NOUN) [rəʊ] (**rəu**) UK, [roʊ] (**roh**) US is a line of objects.

(VERB) [rəʊ] (**rəu**) UK, [roʊ] (**roh**) US; pronounced as the above, but is unrelated to it and means "to propel a boat in water a using oars").

(NOUN) [raʊ] (**raau**) is a noisy argument (to [raʊ] (raau) means "to argue noisily").

By the way, J. K. Rowling is pronounced ['rəʊlɪŋ] (**rəu**-ling).

sow

(VERB) [səʊ] (**səu**) UK, [soʊ] (**soh**) US means "to scatter plant seeds" (you can sow a field, for example) and it is pronounced exactly the same as "to sew" (i.e. as "so", not as "Sue") which means "to use thread and a needle to join two pieces of fabric".

(NOUN) [saʊ] (**saau**) is a female pig.

mow

(VERB) [məʊ] (**məu**) UK, [moʊ] (**moh**) US means "to cut down" (usually a lawn).

(NOUN) [maʊ] (**maau**) is the place in a barn where hay is stored.

sewer

(NOUN) [ˈsuːəʳ] (**soo**-ə) or [ˈsjuːəʳ] (**syoo**-ə) UK, [ˈsuːɚ] (**soo**-rr) US is a pipe used to remove liquid human waste.

(NOUN) [ˈsəʊəʳ] (**səu**-ə) UK, [ˈsoʊɚ] (**soh**-rr) US is someone who sews (səuz resp. soh'z, see above).

close

(VERB) [kləʊz] (**kləuz**) UK, [kloʊz] (**kloh'z**) US is the opposite of "to open".

(ADJ) [kləʊs] (**kləus**) UK, [kloʊs] (**kloh's**) US (notice the "s" at the end) is an adjective meaning "near".

Polish

(VERB) [ˈpʰɒlɪʃ] (**poll-ish**) UK, [ˈpʰɑːlɪʃ] (**paa-lish**) US means "to make a surface smooth".

(ADJ/NOUN) [ˈpʰəʊlɪʃ] (**pəu**-lish) UK, [ˈpʰoʊlɪʃ] (**poh**-lish) refers to the language or the nation based in Poland [ˈpʰəʊlənd] (**pəu**-lənd) UK, [ˈpʰoʊlənd] (**poh**-lənd) US.

lead

(VERB) [liːd] (**leed**) means "to guide or conduct" ([liːd] can also be a noun meaning "the act of leading").

(NOUN) [lɛd] (**led**) is a chemical element with the symbol "Pb" ("plumbum" in Latin).

graduate

(NOUN) [ˈɡrædʒuət] (**grædzh**-u-ət) is a person holding an academic degree.

(VERB) [ˈɡrædʒueɪt] (**grædzh**-u-eyt) means to obtain an academic degree. Notice that although the pronunciation is different, there is no difference in stress position.

does

(VERB) [dʌz] (**dʌz**) is the third person of the verb "to do".

(NOUN) [dəʊz] (**dəuz**) UK, [doʊz] (**doh'z**) US is the plural form of the noun "doe" (a female deer).

bass

(NOUN) [beɪs] (**beys**) is the lowest voice in a harmony ("beys" is also an adjective meaning "low sounding");

(NOUN) [bæs] (**bæs**) is a member of a certain species of fish.

number

(NOUN) [ˈnʌmbəʳ] (**nʌm**-bə) UK, [ˈnʌmbɚ] (**nʌm**-br) US is a mathematical object such as 1, 65536, 3.1415.

(ADJ) [ˈnʌməʳ] (**nʌ**-mə) UK, [ˈnʌmɚ] (**nʌ**-mr) US means "more numb" (numb is pronounced [nʌm] (nʌm)).

dove

(NOUN) [dʌv] (**dʌv**) is a bird related to pigeons.

(VERB) [dəʊv] (**dəuv**) UK, [doʊv] (**doh'v**) US is a non-standard form of the past tense of the verb "to dive" used in some dialects (the standard one is "dived").

house

(NOUN) [haʊs] (**haaus**) is a building.

(VERB) [haʊz] (**haauz**) means "to provide place to live". Notice the "z" at the end.

slough

(NOUN) [slaʊ] (**slaau**) is a state of sadness with no hope, or a soft wet area of land.

(VERB) [slʌf] (**slʌf**) means "to get rid of a layer of dead skin", for example snakes slough.

ornament

(NOUN) [ˈɔːnəmənt] (*aw*-nə-mənt) UK, [ˈɔːrnəmənt] (*awr*-nə-mənt) US is an object used for decoration.

(VERB) [ˈɔːnəˌmɛnt] (*aw*-nə-ment) UK, [ˈɔːrnəmɛnt] (*awr*-nə-ment) US means "to add decoration to something".

implement

(NOUN) [ˈɪmpləmənt] (**im**-plə-mənt) is a tool or an instrument.

(VERB) [ˈɪmpləˌmɛnt] (**im**-plə-ment) means "to make something start happening or being used";

II.6 STRESS POSITION AND MEANING

As we have seen in the previous section, English orthography contains a lot of ambiguities. There is one very large class of heteronyms characterized by shifting of the stress position in a word. Sometimes the distinction is present only in some dialects; the list below contains only those that are common in either standard American English or standard British English (and usually in both). Brace yourselves; there are more than 100 such words.

absent; [ˈæbsənt] (**æb**-sənt) (ADJ) means "not present"; [æbˈsɛnt] (æb-**sent**) (VERB) is mostly used in the phrase "to absent yourself" meaning "not to go to a place where one is expected to be".

accent; [ˈæksənt] (**æk**-sənt) (NOUN) is the way people in a particular area speak; [əkˈsɛnt] (ək-**sent**) (VERB) (MOSTLY UK) means "to emphasize" (it is often pronounced the same as the noun in American English).

addict; [ˈædɪkt] (**æ**-dikt) (NOUN) is a person addicted to something (such as heroin); [əˈdɪkt] (ə-**dikt**) means "to cause someone to become addicted".

address; [ˈædrɛs] (**æ**-dres) (NOUN) (US ONLY) is the name of the place where you live; [əˈdrɛs] (ə-**dres**) (VERB) means "to direct a speech to someone" (in the UK, both meanings are usually pronounced [əˈdrɛs] (ə-**dres**)).

affect; [əˈfɛkt] (ə-**fekt**) (VERB) means "to influence"; [ˈæfɛkt] (**æ**-fekt) (NOUN) is used in psychology for "a subjective feeling experienced in response to a stimulus".

affix; [ˈæfɪks] (**æ**-fiks) (NOUN) is a grammatical term for a group of letters added to a root word; [əˈfɪks] (ə-**fiks**) (VERB) means "to attach".

alloy; [ˈælɔɪ] (**æ**-loy) (NOUN) is a mixture of metals; [əˈlɔɪ] (ə-**loy**) (VERB) means "to mix metals".

ally; [ˈælaɪ] (**æ**-laay) (NOUN) is a country that supports another country; [əˈlaɪ] (ə-**laay**) (VERB) means "to give your support to another country".

attribute; [ˈætrɪbjuːt] (**æ**-trib-yoot) (NOUN) is a characteristics of something; [əˈtrɪbjuːt] (ə-**trib**-yoot) (VERB) means "to express that something was created by someone".

combine; [kəmˈbaɪn] (kəm-**baayn**) (VERB) means "to bring together"; [ˈkɒmbaɪn] (**komm**-baayn) UK, [ˈkɑːmbaɪn] (**kaam**-baayn) US (NOUN) is a shorter name for a "combine harvester".

commune; [ˈkɒmjuːn] (**komm**-yoon) UK, [ˈkɑːmjuːn] (**kaam**-yoon) US (NOUN) is a group of people living together and sharing responsibilities; [kəˈmjuːn] (kə-**myoon**) (VERB) is used in "commune with somebody" which means "to silently share emotions with somebody".

compact; [ˈkɒmpækt] (**komm**-pækt) UK, [ˈkɑːmpækt] (**kaam**-pækt) US (ADJ) means "including many things in a small space"; [kəmˈpækt] (kəm-**pækt**) (VERB) means "to compress".

complex; [ˈkɒmplɛks] (**komm**-pleks) UK, [ˈkɑːmplɛks] (**kaam**-pleks) US (NOUN) is a (psychological) problem or a collection of buildings; in some dialects (both in British and American English) the adjective "complex" meaning "not simple" is pronounced as [kəmˈplɛks] (kəm-**pleks**); in others, it is pronounced the same as the noun.

compound; [ˈkɒmpaʊnd] (**komm**-paaund) UK, [ˈkɑːmpaʊnd] (**kaam**-paaund) US (NOUN) is a thing consisting of two or more separate parts (or an adjective describing such a thing); [kəmˈpaʊnd] (kəm-**paaund**) (VERB) means "to make something that is already bad become even worse", usually used in the passive as "to be compounded". "To be compounded" can also mean "to be formed from".

compress; [kəmˈprɛs] (kəm-**pres**) (VERB) means "to press or squeeze together"; [ˈkɒmprɛs] (**komm**-pres) UK, [ˈkɑːmprɛs] (**kaam**-pres) US (NOUN) is a piece of cloth applied to a body part to reduce pain (a cold compress), reduce muscle fatigue (a warm compress) etc.

conduct; [kənˈdʌkt] (kən-**dʌkt**) (VERB) means "to manage, carry on" (e.g. "to conduct a meeting") or "to lead" (e.g. "to conduct an orchestra). [ˈkɒndʌkt] (**konn**-dʌkt) UK, [ˈkɑːndʌkt] (**kaan**-dʌkt) US (NOUN) is a person's behaviour.

confine(s); [kənˈfaɪn] (kən-**faayn**) (VERB) means "to keep somebody or something within certain limits"; [ˈkɒnfaɪnz] (**kon**-faaynz) UK, [ˈkɑːnfaɪnz] (**kaan**-faaynz) US (NOUN) is used only in the plural and means "limits, borders" (for example "confines of human knowledge").

conflict; [ˈkɒnflɪkt] (**konn**-flikt) UK, [ˈkɑːnflɪkt] (**kaan**-flikt) US (NOUN) means "a disagreement"; [kənˈflɪkt] (kən-**flikt**) (VERB) means "to be incompatible with".

conscript; [ˈkɒnskrɪpt] UK, [ˈkɑːnskrɪpt] US (NOUN) is someone who compulsorily joined the armed forces of a country; [kənˈskrɪpt] (VERB) means "to become a conscript".

conserve; [kənˈsɜːv] (kən-**sə'əv**) UK, [kənˈsɝːv] (kən-**sərv**) US (VERB) means "to use as little as possible" (e.g. "to conserve energy") or "to protect something from being destroyed" (e.g. "to conserve wildlife"); [ˈkɒnsɜːv] (**konn**-sə'əv) UK, [ˈkɑːnsɝːv] (**kaan**-sərv) US

(NOUN) is synonymous to "whole fruit jam". Unlike in other languages, it *isn't* synonymous to a can (an aluminium container).

console; ['kɒnsəʊl] (**konn**-səul) UK or ['kɑːnsoʊl] (**kaan**-soh'l) US (NOUN) is "a cabinet (often for a TV) designed to stand on the floor" or "a device for playing video games"; [kənˈsəʊl] (kən-**səul**) UK or [kənˈsoʊl] (kən-**soh'l**) US (VERB) means "to make someone feel better".

consort; ['kɒnsɔːt] (**konn**-saw't) UK, ['kɑːnsɔːrt] (**kaan**-saw'rt) US (NOUN) is used mainly in "the queen consort", meaning "the wife of a king", and "the prince consort", meaning "the husband of a queen" (rarely also "the king consort"), and sometimes also "the princess consort", meaning "the wife of a prince"; [kənˈsɔːt] (kən-**saw't**) UK, [kənˈsɔːrt] (kən-**saw'rt**) US means "to spend time in someone's company", usually meant contemptuously, for example "the duke consorted with prostitutes".

construct; [kənˈstrʌkt] (kən-**strʌkt**) (VERB) means "to build"; ['kɒnstrʌkt] (**konn**-strʌkt) UK or ['kɑːnstrʌkt] (**kaan**-strʌkt) US (NOUN) is something constructed or a concept.

consult; [kənˈsʌlt] (kən-**sʌlt**) (VERB) means "to seek opinion or advice"; ['kɒnsʌlt] (**konn**-sʌlt) UK, ['kɑːnsʌlt] (**kaan**-sʌlt) US (NOUN) is an obsolete term meaning a decision or an agreement, or, in the US, also "a visit" (e.g. to a doctor).

content; ['kɒntɛnt] (**konn**-tent) UK, ['kɑːntɛnt] (**kaan**-tent) US (NOUN) is "the contained material"; [kənˈtɛnt] (kən-**tent**) (ADJ) means "satisfied" (it can also be a verb meaning "to satisfy").

contest; ['kɒntɛst] (**konn**-test) UK, ['kɑːntɛst] (**kaan**-test) US (NOUN) is a competition; [kənˈtɛst] (kən-**test**) (VERB) is used in "to contest something" which means "to take part in something in order to win", or it can mean "to formally oppose something", for example "to contest a will".

contract; [ˈkɒntrækt] (**konn**-trækt) UK, [ˈkɑːntrækt] (**kaan**-trækt) US (NOUN) is an official agreement; [kənˈtrækt] (kən-**trækt**) (VERB) is the opposite to "expand", or it can mean "to get an illness" (e.g. "to contract AIDS").

contrast; [ˈkɒntrɑːst] (**konn**-traast) UK, [ˈkɑːntræst] (**kaan**-træst) US (NOUN) is "a difference in brightness"; [kənˈtrɑːst] (kən-**traast**) UK, [kənˈtræst] (kən-**træst**) US (VERB) means "to show the difference" (in some US dialects, both meanings are pronounced as the noun given here).

converse; [kənˈvɜːs] (kən-**vəˈəs**) UK, [kənˈvɜːs] (kən-**vərs**) US (VERB) means "to have a conversation"; [ˈkɒnvɜːs] (**konn**-vəˈəs) UK, [ˈkɑːn-vɜːs] (**kaan**-vərs) US (NOUN) is the opposite or reverse of something.

convert; [kənˈvɜːt] (kən-**vəˈət**) UK, [kənˈvɜːt] (kən-**vərt**) US (VERB) means "to change something from one form to another"; [ˈkɒn-vɜːt] (**konn**-vəˈət) UK, [ˈkɑːnvɜːt] (**kaan**-vəˈət) US (NOUN) is a person who changed his or her religion.

convict; [kənˈvɪkt] (kən-**vikt**) (VERB) means "to find someone guilty in court"; [ˈkɒnvɪkt] (**konn**-vikt) UK, [ˈkɑːnvɪkt] (**kaan**-vikt) US (NOUN) is a person who has been convicted.

decrease; [dɪˈkriːs] (dik-**rees**) (VERB) means "to become smaller"; [ˈdiːkriːs] (**dee**-krees) (NOUN) is "a reduction".

defect; [dɪˈfɛkt] (di-**fekt**) (VERB) is used in "to defect from" which means "to leave a group to join an enemy", for example "to defect from a political party before elections"; [ˈdiːfɛkt] (**dee**-fekt) (NOUN) is a fault that makes something imperfect (but the same pronunciation as for the verb is also common).

desert; [ˈdɛzət] (**dez**-ət) UK, [ˈdɛzɚt] (**dez**-rt) US (NOUN) is a large area of dry land; [dɪˈzɜːt] (di-**zə'ət**) UK, [dɪˈzɜːt] (di-**zərt**) US (VERB) means "to abandon something".

invalid; [ɪnˈvælɪd] (in-**væ**-lid) (ADJ) is the opposite of "valid"; [ˈɪn-vəlɪd] (**in**-və-lid) or [ˈɪnvəliːd] (**in**-və-leed) (NOUN) is a person that needs others who take care of him or her. The latter pronunciation can also be a verb meaning "to force somebody to leave armed forces because of injury".

detail; [ˈdiːteɪl] (**dee**-teyl) (NOUN) is "something small or negligible enough"; in the US, [dɪˈteɪl] (di-**teyl**) is a verb meaning "to explain in detail" (in the UK the verb sounds the same as the noun).

dictate; [dɪkˈteɪt] (dik-**teyt**) (VERB) means "to say something for someone else to write down" (for example "to dictate a letter to a secretary") or "to tell somebody what to do"; [ˈdɪkteɪt] (**dik**-teyt) (NOUN) is a rule that one must obey.

digest; [daɪˈdʒɛst] (daay-**dzhest**) or [dɪˈdʒɛst] (di-**dzhest**) means "to change food to a form the body can use" (e.g. "humans cannot digest grass") or "to think about something in order to understand it"; [ˈdaɪdʒɛst] (**daay**-dzhest) (NOUN) is a short report containing the most important information.

discard; [dɪsˈkɑːd] (dis-**kaad**) UK, [dɪsˈkɑːrd] (dis-**kaard**) US means "to get rid of something one no longer needs"; [ˈdɪskɑːd] (**dis**-kaad) UK, [ˈdɪskɑːrd] (**dis**-kaard) US (NOUN) is a thing no longer wanted and thrown away (usually in a card game).

discharge; [dɪsˈtʃɑːdʒ] (dis-**tchaadzh**) UK, [dɪsˈtʃɑːrdʒ] (dis-**tchaardzh**) US (VERB) means "to release" (for example, "to discharge someone from a hospital" means "to give him official permission to leave"); [ˈdɪstʃɑːdʒ] (**dis**-tchaadzh) UK, [ˈdɪstʃɑːrdʒ] (**dis**-tchaardzh) US (NOUN) is the act of releasing, for example "a discharge of toxic waste".

discount; [ˈdɪskaʊnt] (**dis**-kaaunt) (NOUN) is the amount of money which something costs less than usual; [dɪsˈkaʊnt] (dis-**kaaunt**) (VERB) means either "to reduce price of something" or "to dismiss, to consider something unimportant", as in "we cannot discount the possibility of further attacks" (in the US, the verb is sometimes pronounced the same as the noun).

discourse; [ˈdɪskɔːs] (**dis**-kaw's) UK, [ˈdɪskɔːrs] (**dis**-kaw'rs) US (NOUN) is a serious discussion; [dɪsˈkɔːs] (dis-**kaw's**) UK, [dɪsˈkɔːrs] (dis-**kaw'rs**) US (VERB) means "to talk long about a subject you know well".

escort; [ɪˈskɔːt] (ih-**skaw't**) UK, [ɪˈskɔːrt] (ih-**skaw'rt**) US (VERB) means "to go with somebody in order to protect or guard them"; [ˈɛskɔːt] (**es**-kaw't) UK, [ˈɛskɔːrt] (**es**-kaw'rt) US (NOUN) is a person or a group of people who escort somebody.

essay; [ˈɛseɪ] (**es**-ey) (NOUN) is a short piece of writing by a student; [ɛˈseɪ] (es-**ey**) (VERB) is a literary term meaning "to try to do".

excise; [ɪkˈsaɪz] (ik-**saayz**) (VERB) means "to remove completely"; [ˈɛksaɪz] (**ek**-saayz) is a tax on specific goods.

exploit; [ɪkˈsplɔɪt] (ik-**semploy**t) (VERB) means "to use someone or something for your own advantage"; [ˈɛksplɔɪt] (**ek**-sployt) (NOUN) is a brave or interesting act.

export; [ɪksˈpɔːt] (iks-**paw't**) UK, [ɪksˈpɔːrt] (iks-**paw'rt**) US (VERB) means "to sell goods to a foreign country"; [ˈɛkspɔːt] (**ek**-spaw't) UK or [ˈɛkspɔːrt] (**ek**-spaw'rt) US (NOUN) is "something that is exported".

extract; [ɪksˈtrækt] (iks-**trækt**) (VERB) means "to get something out of something else"; [ˈɛkstrækt] (**eks**-trækt) (NOUN) is "something extracted".

ferment; [fəˈmɛnt] (fə-**ment**) UK, [fɚˈmɛnt] (fr-**ment**) US (VERB) means "to experience a chemical change because of the action of yeasts"; [ˈfɜːmɛnt] (**fə'ə**-ment) UK, [ˈfɜːmɛnt] (**fər**-ment) US (NOUN) is a state of political and social confusion and excitement (for example a country can be in ferment).

frequent; [ˈfriːkwənt] (**free**-kwənt) (ADJ) means "happening often"; [friˈkwɛnt] (frik-**went**) (VERB) means "to visit often".

gallant; [ˈɡælənt] (**gæl**-ənt) (ADJ); a man is gallant if he gives polite attention to women; [ɡəˈlænt] (ɡə-**lænt**) (NOUN) is an old-fashioned term for a man that is gallant (it is sometimes also pronounced the same as the adjective).

impact; [ˈɪmpækt] (**im**-pækt) (NOUN) is "a forceful collision"; [ɪmˈpækt] (im-**pækt**) (VERB) means "to affect".

implant; [ɪmˈplɑːnt] (im-**plaant**) UK, [ɪmˈplænt] (im-**plænt**) US (VERB) means "to fix firmly" or "to insert into the body"; [ˈɪmplɑːnt] (**im**-plaant) UK, [ˈɪmplænt] (**im**-plænt) US (NOUN) is "something surgically implanted in the body".

import; [ɪmˈpɔːt] (im-**paw't**) UK, [ɪmˈpɔːrt] (im-**paw'rt**) US (VERB) means "to bring a product from another country to one's own country"; [ˈɪmpɔːt] (im-pawˈt) UK, [ˈɪmpɔːrt] (im-pawˈrt) US (NOUN) is the act of importing a product (or the product itself).

impress; [ɪmˈprɛs] (im-**pres**) (VERB) means "to make someone feel admiration for you"; [ˈɪmprɛs] (**im**-pres) (NOUN) is the act of impressing.

imprint; [ˈɪmprɪnt] (**im**-print) (NOUN) is a mark made by stamping something onto a surface; [ɪmˈprɪnt] (im-**print**) (VERB) means "to have a great effect on something".

incense; [ˈɪnsɛns] (**in**-sens) (NOUN) is a substance producing a pleasant smell when it is burning (it is often used in churches, for example); [ɪnˈsɛns] (in-**sens**) (VERB) means "to get somebody very angry".

incline; [ɪnˈklaɪn] (in-**klaayn**) (VERB) means "to behave in a particular way"; [ˈɪnklaɪn] (**in**-klaayn) (NOUN) is a slope.

increase; [ɪnˈkriːs] (in-**krees**) (VERB) means "to become larger"; [ˈɪnkriːs] (**in**-krees) (NOUN) is "an amount by which something increased".

indent; [ɪnˈdɛnt] (in-**dent**) (VERB) means "to start a line of text further from the edge than other lines"; [ˈɪndɛnt] (**in**-dent) (NOUN) is an official order for goods or equipment.

inlay; [ɪnˈleɪ] (in-**lei**) (VERB) means "to decorate the surface of something by putting pieces of wood or metal into it in such a way that the resulting surface remains smooth"; [ˈɪnleɪ] (**in**-lei) (NOUN) is a pattern of such a decoration.

insert; [ɪnˈsɜːt] (in-**səˈət**) UK, [ɪnˈsɜːt] (in-**sert**) US (VERB) means "to put something into something else"; [ˈɪnsɜːt] (**in**-səˈət) UK, [ˈɪnsɜːt] (in-sərt) US (NOUN) is usually an extra section added to a newspaper or magazine (but it can mean something that is put into something else in general).

insult; [ɪnˈsʌlt] (in-**sʌlt**) (VERB) means "to offend someone"; [ˈɪnsʌlt] (**in**-sʌlt) (NOUN) is an action intended to be rude.

interchange; [ˈɪntətʃeɪndʒ] (**in**-tə-tcheyndzh) UK, [ˈɪntəˑtʃeɪndʒ] (**in**-tr-tcheyndzh) UK (NOUN) is the act of sharing or exchanging something; [ˌɪntəˈtʃeɪndʒ] (in-tə-**tcheyndzh**) UK, [ˌɪntəˑˈtʃeɪndʒ] (in-tr-**tcheyndzh**) US (VERB) means "to share or exchange ideas".

intern; [ɪnˈtɜːn] (in-**tə'ən**) UK, [ɪnˈtɜːn] (in-**tərn**) US (VERB) means "to put somebody in prison during a war without charging them with a crime"; [ˈɪntɜːn] (**in**-tə'ən) UK, [ˈɪntɜːn] (**in**-tərn) US (NOUN) is a student of medicine working at a hospital to get further experience.

invite; [ɪnˈvaɪt] (in-**vaayt**) (VERB) means "to ask somebody to come to a social event"; [ˈɪnvaɪt] (**in**-vaayt) is an informal word for "invitation".

mismatch; [ˈmɪsmætʃ] (**mis**-mætch) (NOUN) is a combination of things that do not go well together; [ˌmɪsˈmætʃ] (mis-**mætch**) (VERB) means "to fail to match".

object; [ˈɒbdʒɪkt] (**obb**-dzhikt) UK or [ˈɑːbdʒɪkt] (**aab**-dzhikt) US (NOUN) is a thing or the goal of something; [əbˈdʒɛkt] (əb-**dzhekt**) (VERB) means "to disagree with something".

overlap; [ˌəʊvəˈlæp] (əu-və-**læp**) UK, [ˌoʊvəˈlæp] (*oh*-vr-**læp**) US (VERB); if two things overlap, part of one thing covers part of the other; [ˈəʊvəlæp] (**əu**-və-læp) UK, [ˈoʊvəlæp] (*oh*-vr-læp) US (NOUN) is a shared area (between two objects).

overlay; [ˈəʊvəleɪ] (əu-və-lei) UK, [ˈoʊvɚleɪ] (oh-vr-lei) US (NOUN) is something put on top of something else; [ˌəʊvəˈleɪ] (əu-və-**lei**) UK, [ˌoʊvɚˈleɪ] (oh-vr-**lei**) US (VERB) means "to put something on top of the surface of something else".

perfect; [ˈpɜːfɪkt] (**pə'ə**-fikt) UK, [ˈpɜːfɪkt] (**pər**-fikt) US (ADJ) means "excellent; precise"; [pəˈfɛkt] (pə-**fekt**) UK or [pəˈfɛkt] (pr-**fekt**) US (VERB) means "to make perfect".

permit; [pəˈmɪt] (pə-**mit**) UK, [pɚˈmɪt] (pr-**mit**) US (VERB) means "to allow"; [ˈpɜːmɪt] (**pə'ə**-mit) UK, [ˈpɜːmɪt] (**pər**-mit) US (NOUN) is an official document that gives somebody the right to do something.

pervert; [ˈpɜːvɜːt] (**pə'ə**-və'ət) UK, [ˈpɜːvɜːt] (**pər**-vərt) US (NOUN) is someone whose sexual behaviour is considered unacceptable; [pəˈvɜːt] (pə-**və'ət**) UK, [pɚˈvɜːt] (pr-**vərt**) US (VERB) means "to change something in a bad way".

present; [ˈprɛzənt] (**prez**-ənt) is either an adjective meaning "relating to now" or "located in the vicinity" or a noun meaning either "the current period of time" or "a gift"; [prɪˈzɛnt] (pri-**zent**) is a verb meaning "to show".

proceed(s); [prəˈsiːd] (prə-**seed**) UK, [proʊˈsiːd] (proh-**seed**) US (VERB) means "to continue doing something"; [ˈprəʊsiːdz] (**prəu**-seedz) UK, [ˈproʊsiːdz] (**proh**-seedz) US (NOUN) is used only in the plural form as "proceeds of" meaning "revenue from", e.g. "proceeds of the concert went to charity".

produce; [prəˈdjuːs] (prə-**dyoos**) UK, [prəˈduːs] (prə-**doos**) US (VERB) means "to make or grow something"; [ˈprɒdjuːs] (**prodd**-yoos) UK, [ˈprɑːduːs] (**praa**-doos) or [ˈproʊduːs] (**proh**-doos) US (NOUN) means "things that have been produced", usually in connection with farming.

progress; ['prəʊgrɛs] (**prəu**-gres) UK or ['prɑːgrɛs] (**praa**-gres) US (NOUN) means "a development of something"; [prə'grɛs] (prə-**gres**) (VERB) means "to advance".

project; ['prɒdʒɛkt] (**prodzh**-ekt) UK, ['prɑːdʒɛkt] (**praa**-dzhekt) US (NOUN) is "something that is planned"; [prə'dʒɛkt] (prə-**dzhekt**) (VERB) means "to plan something".

protest; ['prəʊtɛst] (**prəu**-test) UK, ['proʊtɛst] (**proh**-test) US (NOUN) is an expression of disagreement with something; [prə'tɛst] (prə-**test**) (VERB) means "to express disagreement" (it can also be pronounced the same as the noun in the US).

purport; [pə'pɔːt] (pə-**paw't**) UK, [pə-'pɔːrt] (pr-**paw'rt**) US (VERB) is used especially in "purport to be something" which means "to claim to be something" (for example this book does **not** purport to be able to teach you everything you will ever need to know about English); ['pɜːpɔːt] (**pə'ə**-paw't) UK, ['pɜːˌpɔːrt] (**pər**-paw'rt) US (NOUN); the "purport of something" is "the general meaning of something".

rebel; [rɪ'bɛl] (ri-**bel**) (VERB) means "to fight against authority"; ['rɛbəl] (**reb**-əl) (NOUN) is someone who rebels against something.

recoil; [rɪ'kɔɪl] (ri-**koyl**) (VERB) means "to move your body quickly away from something because you find it frightening"; ['riːkɔɪl] (**ree**-koyl) (NOUN) is a sudden movement backwards.

record; ['rɛkɔːd] (**rek**-aw'd) UK, ['rɛkəd] (**rek**-rd) US (NOUN) is "an information put into a physical medium" or "the extreme value of an achievement (in sport)"; [rɪ'kɔːd] (ri-**kaw'd**) UK, [rə'kɔrd] (rə-**kaw'rd**) US (VERB) means "to make a recording of something".

refill; [ˌriːˈfɪl] (ree-**fil**) (VERB) means "to fill something again"; [ˈriːfɪl] (**ree**-fil) (NOUN) is something used to refill a container; also, it means "another drink of the same type".

refund; [ˈriːfʌnd] (**ree**-fʌnd) (NOUN) is a sum of money to be paid back; [rɪˈfʌnd] (ri-**fʌnd**) (VERB) means "to give somebody back their money for something they bought".

refuse; [rɪˈfjuːz] (ri-**fyooz**) (VERB) means "disallow something"; [ˈrɛfjuːs] (**ref**-yoos) (NOUN) is waste material.

reject; [rɪˈdʒɛkt] (ri-**dzhekt**) (VERB) means "to refuse something"; [ˈriːdʒɛkt] (**ree**-dzhekt) (NOUN) is something that cannot be used because it is faulty or someone who is not considered member of a team, society etc.

remake; [ˈriːmeɪk] (**ree**-meyk) (NOUN) is a new version of an old film or song; [ˌriːˈmeɪk] (ree-**meyk**) (VERB) means "to create a remake".

reprint; [ˌriːˈprɪnt] (ree-**print**) (VERB) means "to print (usually a book) again without changes"; [ˈriːprɪnt] (**ree**-print) (NOUN) is a book that has been reprinted.

retake; [ˌriːˈteɪk] (ree-**teyk**) (VERB) is used especially in military; it means "to take control of something (e.g. a town) again"; [ˈriːteɪk] (**ree**-teyk) (NOUN) is the act of filming a scene again, because the first take was not good enough.

retard; [rɪˈtɑːd] (ri-**taad**) UK, [rɪˈtɑːrd] (ri-**taard**) US (VERB) means "to make something progress slower"; [ˈriːtɑːd] (**ree**-taad) UK, [ˈriːtɑːrd] (**ree**-taard) US (NOUN) is a slang term for a mentally retarded person.

segment; [ˈsɛgmənt] (**seg**-mənt) (NOUN) is a part of something (and also a geometric figure consisting of two points connected by a straight line); [sɛgˈment] (seg-**ment**) (VERB) means "to divide into segments".

subject; [ˈsʌbdʒɪkt] (**sʌb**-dzhikt) or [ˈsʌbdʒɛkt] (**sʌb**-dzhekt) (NOUN) is a thing or person being discussed (it can also be an adjective used in "subject to something" which means "to be affected by something"); [səbˈdʒɛkt] (səb-**dzhekt**) (VERB) means "to bring a country under control" (for example "Germany subjected most of Europe during WWII"); "to be subjected to something" means "to be affected by something".

survey; [ˈsɜːveɪ] (**sə'ə**-vei) UK, [ˈsɜːveɪ] (**sər**-vei) US (NOUN) is finding opinions of people by asking questions; [səˈveɪ] (sə-**vei**) UK, [səˈveɪ] (sr-**vei**) US (VERB) means "to look carefully at something".

suspect; [səˈspɛkt] (sə-**spekt**) (VERB) means "to think that somebody or something is guilty of something without having a definite proof"; [ˈsʌspɛkt] (**sʌs**-pekt) (NOUN) is a person who is suspected of a crime.

torment; [tɔːˈmɛnt] (taw-**ment**) UK, [tɔːrˈmɛnt] (taw'r-**ment**) US (VERB) means "to make somebody suffer"; [ˈtɔːmɛnt] (**taw**-ment) UK, [ˈtɔːrmɛnt] (**taw'r**-ment) US (NOUN) is extreme suffering.

transfer; [trænsˈfɜː'] (træns-fə'**ə**) UK, [trænsˈfɜː] (træns-**fər**) US (VERB) means "to move from one place to another"; [ˈtrænsfɜː'] (**træns**-ə'ə) UK, [ˈtrænsfɜː] (**træns**-fər) US (NOUN) is the act of moving somebody from one place to another.

transplant; [trænsˈplɑːnt] (træns-**plaant**) UK, [trænsˈplænt] (træns-**plænt**) US (VERB) means "to take an organ from one organism and put it into another"; [ˈtrænsplɑːnt] (**træns**-plaant) UK, [ˈtrænsplænt] (**træns**-plænt) US (NOUN) is either an operation during which a an organ is transplanted or the organ that is being transplanted.

transport; [træn'spɔːt] (træn-**spaw't**) UK, [træn'spɔːrt] (træn-**spaw'rt**) US (VERB) means "to take something from one place to another"; ['trænspɔːt] (**træn**-spaw't) UK, ['trænspɔːrt] (**træn**-spaw'rt) US (NOUN) is a system for carrying people or things from one place to another.

traverse; [trə'vɜːs] (trə-**və'əs**) UK, [trə'vɜːs] (trə-**vərs**) US (VERB) means "to cross an area"; ['trævɜːs] (**træ**-və'əs) UK, ['trævɜːs] (**træ**-vərs) US (NOUN) is a term used in mountain climbing and means "an act of moving across a steep slope".

update; [ˌʌp'deɪt] (ʌp-**deyt**) (VERB) means "to bring something up to date"; ['ʌpdeɪt] (**ʌp**-deyt) (NOUN) is a report that gives the most recent information on something; in computing it means also a package containing improvements for a software.

upgrade; [ʌp'greɪd] (ʌp-**greyd**) (VERB) means to "make something better or more advanced"; ['ʌpgreɪd] (**ʌp**-greyd) (NOUN) is the new part that makes it better.

uplift; [ˌʌp'lɪft] (ʌp-**lift**) (VERB) means "to make somebody feel happier"; ['ʌplɪft] (**ʌp**-lift) (NOUN) is the act of something being raised.

upset; [ʌp'sɛt] (ʌp-**set**) (VERB) means "to make somebody feel unhappy" (it is also an adjective meaning "unhappy or angry"); ['ʌpsɛt] (**ʌp**-set) (NOUN) is a situation connected with difficulties.

II.7 Alphabetical index of Part II

PART III

ENGLISH PHONOLOGY

III.1 **IPA** FOR **ENGLISH**

The International Phonetic Alphabet (IPA) has become standard when denoting English pronunciation, and proper knowledge of it is essential for any learner who wants to further improve his or her pronunciation. It is based on the Latin alphabet (the standard English alphabet); each letter of the alphabet is assigned a particular sound, and many other characters (e.g. ʃ, ʒ, ɔ) are added to the alphabet in order to be able to, theoretically, denote any sound that occurs in any language in the world to quite a high degree of precision.

Unlike some other phonetic alphabets, there is no way to recognize what exact sound an IPA symbol represents just from its symbol. On the other hand, the symbols are usually chosen so that similar symbols denote similar sounds, so, for example, [ɔ] sounds similar to "o", which helps you associate the symbol with the correct pronunciation. In this chapter we shall take a look only at the symbols used to denote English pronunciation.

We will use two technical terms in this chapter: an **open syllable** is a syllable that ends with a vowel (in writing, so for example "ta" in "take" = "ta-ke" would be open), and **closed syllable** is a syllable that ends with a consonant (again in writing; for example all vowels followed by a double letter constitute a closed syllable, as in "written" = "writ-ten").

Remark: When I write "most languages" in this section, I mean "most languages that use the Latin alphabet".

VOWELS

[Xː] long vowel

When the symbol "ː" follows a vowel symbol, it means that the vowel is pronounced longer.

['XY] stressed syllable

This symbol, which looks similar to an apostrophe, means that the following syllable is stressed (it is pronounced louder).

[,XY] secondary stress

This symbol, which looks similar to a comma, is basically the same as the above, only the stress is weaker.

[æ] cat, bad, sad, sand, land, hand

Among all the English vowels, the greatest problem for most learners poses "æ". It is somewhere in between of "a" in "father" and "e" in "bed". It is usually pronounced slightly longer and closer to "e" in "bed" in American English, whereas it is often shorter and closer to "a" in "father" in British English. It is always represented by the letter "a" in a stressed closed syllable, but not all such occurrences are pronounced as [æ].

In some American dialects, it is pronounced approximately [ɛə] which may lead to confusion (words like "bad" and "bed" may sound the same to someone not used to the dialect), even among native speakers.

[ɑː] bra, calm, palm, f<u>a</u>ther, start, dark

This vowel is the closest one to the sound of the letter "a" in many other languages and as such is also denoted [a] in some dictionaries. There is no reliable general rule which would tell you when the letter "a" is pronounced as [ɑː] instead of [æ].

In American English, it is quite rare to pronounce "a" as [ɑː]; it is usually pronounced [æ], as in grass, can't, half, bath etc., all of which are pronounced with [ɑː] in British English. On the other hand, the sound is used in American English in words in which a Brit would say [ɒ] (see below), as in god, pot, top, spot.

[ɒ] god, pot, top, spot (British English only)

This vowel is quite similar to the sound of "o" many other languages. It is always represented by "o" in a closed stressed syllable, although such an "o" can also be pronounced differently (e.g. in "come"). Americans don't use this vowel and say [ɑː] instead.

[ʌ] but, cut, gun, come, some, glove

This vowel very similar to [ɑː], but it's never pronounced long in English. It is always represented by "u" in a stressed closed syllable, or by an "o", but both can be pronounced also in a different way.

[ɛ] get, bed, set, sell, fell, men

This vowel is the closest one to the sound of the letter "e" in most other languages and is sometimes denoted by [e] in dictionaries. It is usually represented by an "e" in a closed stressed syllable, but often also by "ai", e.g. said, fair, "ae", e.g. bear, pear, and others.

[ɪ] pit, bin, fill, will, village, bullet

In writing, this sound is most commonly represented by "i" in a closed stressed syllable, but also unstressed "a", "e", or "i" is often pronounced as [ɪ]. If you find [ə] (see below) in a dictionary in a word for which you are almost sure that [ɪ] is correct (or conversely), don't worry; in most cases the two possibilities are interchangeable and usage can vary even among different occurrences of the same word pronounced by the same speaker.

[i], [iː] he, she, see, keep, family, hyperbole

This is just a softer [ɪ]. It is mostly represented by "ee" (e.g. seek), but quite often also by "ea" (meat), single "e" (he), final "y" (family) and others. It is usually long when it is in a stressed syllable and short when it is not, but not necessarily.

[ɔː] saw, straw, dawn, fall, call, wall

A similar sound to the British [ɒ], but somewhat "darker". It is usually represented by "aw" (saw) or "al" (talk), but there are many words in which "aw" and "al" is pronounced [ɑː] or [ɔ] in many varieties of American English.

[ʊ] put, full, good, wood, could, would

The sound most similar to the sound of "u" in most other languages. It is often denoted by "u" in a closed stressed syllable (when it is not [ʌ]), but also by "oo" (good), "oul" (could) and other letter groups.

[uː] you, who, chew, shoe, cool, tool

[ʊ] would sound strange if it were long, so when there is a long "u" sound in English, it is pronounced somewhat "darker" than [ʊ]. It is most commonly denoted by "ew" (Jew) and "oo" (tool), but there is no way to tell when "oo" is pronounced as [uː] and when as [ʊ] (this has to be learned by heart).

[ə] a, syllable, moment, terrible, felony, papyrus

Most learners of English learn very fast how to pronounce "a" when it means an indefinite article (such as in "a book"), and this is exactly the pronunciation of [ə]. It can be represented by any vowel (a, e, i, o, u) in an unstressed syllable, see the examples above. When represented by "a" or "i", it is often freely interchangeable with [ɪ]; for example "terrible" can be pronounced either ['tɛrəbl], or ['tɛrɪbl].

Many dictionaries (and this book) use the notation [ᵊ] (i.e. "ə" in the superscript) or [(ə)] to denote [ə] that may be pronounced but doesn't have to be. For example "visible" is pronounced ['vɪzɪbᵊl] which means that some speakers would pronounce it as ['vɪzɪbəl] and others as ['vɪzɪbl]. The two pronunciations are equally acceptable, and even one speaker could use either of them in different situations.

[ɚ] mis**ter**, stand**ar**d, edit**or** (American English only)

This vowel is formed by saying [ə] and at the same time putting your tongue to the position as if you were saying the English "r" (listen to the recordings). It is denoted [ər] in some dictionaries, which is not entirely precise; it is more like a long "r". In all cases where it is used (most notably "-er" at the end of a word), a Brit would say just [ə] or [əʳ] (see below).

[ɜː], [ɝː] **curve, purge, herd, serve, bird, stir**

Don't confuse the symbol with [ɛ]. [ɜː] is pronounced the same as [əː] in some dialects while it is slightly "darker" in others, and some dictionaries don't use it at all and write simply [əː]. The difference between [ɜː] and [ɝː] is the same as between [ə] and [ɚ]. The former is used chiefly in British English, the latter chiefly in American English (listen to the recordings). Dictionaries which denote [ɜː] as [əː] would denote [ɝː] as [əːr] or [ɚː]. In writing, [ɜː] and [ɝː] are usually represented by the letter groups "ur", "er", or "ir".

Consonants

A few technical terms: **voiced consonants** are those in which the vocal chords are active while pronouncing them (e.g. b, v, z, d, g), and **unvoiced consonants** are the others (e.g. p, s, t, k, sh).

[b] **buy, bet, big, hub, knob, superb**

This sound exists in most languages and is also usually denoted by the letter "b". One thing to pay attention to is that it doesn't become "p" when it is at the end of a word (unless it follows an unvoiced consonant). Also, "mb" at the end of a word is pronounced just as "m", as in numb, dumb, lamb.

[d] do, deal, dust, odd, prod, cod

Also a common sound, denoted by "d" in most languages, including English. Again, it doesn't become "t" when it is at the end of a word (unless it follows an unvoiced consonant).

[ð] that, though, there, father, breathe, bathe

A common source of problems for English learners. It is pronounced as if you wanted to say "d" but only slightly touched the back of your teeth by your tongue instead. In particular, it is not pronounced as [d] or [dz]. It is represented by "th" in writing, but "th" is also often [θ] (as in "think", see below), so you will have to learn by heart when to use which one.

[dʒ] jet, joke, giant, purge, huge, banjo

A sound approximately like [d] and [ʒ] (see below) pronounced at the same time. It is usually represented by "j" (which is always pronounced as [dʒ]) or by "g" which is sometimes pronounced as [dʒ] and sometimes as [g] (as in "go"), and there is no general rule to distinguish the two uses.

[f] fast, fat, philosophy, off, stuff, cough

Again, a sound that usually causes little trouble. It is usually represented by "f" or "ph", and also often by "gh" at the end of a word (but "gh" can be pronounced also in many other ways).

[g] go, get, grass, big, dog, fig

The sound similar to "k" but voiced, i.e. with an almost uninterrupted stream of sound coming out of your vocal chords. It is represented by the letter "g", but "g" can by pronounced also many different ways in different contexts. Pay attention to "g" at the end of a word; it is not pronounced as "k" (it stays voiced).

[h] high, how, hot, somehow, ahead, adhere

Native speakers of French and Russian beware! This sound may require some practice. Try to make a neutral sound just by letting air flow through your vocal chords, and then try to "squeeze' the stream of air at the very bottom of your throat. The sound is represented by the letter "h" in writing, but pay attention to all the possible letter groups in which the letter "h" can be present, e.g. "ch", "sh", "th", "gh" etc. It (the sound, not the letter) is never located at the very end of a word or a syllable (there's always at least one vowel after it).

[j] you, yet, yawn, pure, cure, few

The symbol can be slightly confusing, especially for speakers of French and Spanish. In the IPA it represents what is usually written as "y" in English at the beginning of a syllable. It can also appear after another consonant when written as "u", pronounced [jʊ] (e.g. pure), or "ew", pronounced [juː] (e.g. few). Notice: in words like buy [baɪ] and hey [heɪ], the sound at the end is in fact not [j], but the vowel [ɪ] as a part of a diphthong.

[kʰ], [k] keep, cat, character, sock, bloc, cheek

When [k] is at the beginning of a stressed syllable, it is always aspirated (there is always a short "h" after it which is denoted by a superscript "h"). In many dialects, especially in British English, this aspiration can be heard almost for all occurrences of [k] (it doesn't matter by what letter it is represented (such as "k", "c", "ch"), only that there is [k] in pronunciation). If you say [k] in place where [kʰ] is expected, it can lead to a misunderstanding; for example if you pronounce "call" just [kɔːl] instead of [kʰɔːl], some people will think that you said "gall" [gɔːl]. It is, however, never aspirated after "s", e.g. in skin [skin], sky [skaɪ], skate [skeɪt].

Nevertheless, for simplicity, virtually all dictionaries write just [k] and suppose that the reader implicitly understands that it is in fact [kʰ]. This can be very confusing for speakers of languages in which k is not aspirated.

There are many possible ways how [k] can be written: "k", "c", "ch", "ck" and others, but "ch" and "c" can be pronounced also differently and there is no reliable rule to decide when they are pronounced as [k].

[l], [ɫ] low, let, like, owl, cool, well

The sound [ɫ] is called "the dark l". Some dictionaries use [l] to denote pronunciation of the letter "l" that precedes a vowel and [ɫ] otherwise. However, there are some dialects in which an "l" is always dark while in others it is never dark, irrespective of its position. The difference is minor, and it is pointless to worry about it much.

[m] man, my, more, some, doom, seem

This sound is present in almost every language in the world and shouldn't pose any problem. It is always represented by the letter "m".

[n] no, new, nose, ban, soon, keen

Again, no problem here. Speakers of languages in which [n] is often softened to [ɲ] (e.g. Spanish "España", French and German "champignons", Czech "kůň") should pay attention to the pronunciation of words like "new"; which are pronounced with [juː], e.g. [njuː], not [ɲuː].

[ŋ] thing, long, sang, singer, longing, bringing

This sound is produced as if you wanted to say "n" but with the back of your tongue (the part with which you say [g]). It's never at the beginning of a word but can be in the middle of a word derived from a verb by adding "-er" or "-ing" (e.g. singer ['sɪŋəʳ], longing ['lɒŋɪŋ] UK). In other cases when "ng" appears in the middle of a word, it is pronounced [ŋg], as in longer ['lɒŋgəʳ] UK. The letter group "nk" is usually pronounced [ŋk], as in think [θɪŋk], spank [spæŋk].

[pʰ], [p] pit, pale, poke, top, hip, cap

The very same same rules (in terms of aspiration) that hold for "k" hold also for "p". It is always aspirated when it is at the beginning of a stressed syllable and in many dialects also almost everywhere else, except after "s", e.g. spit [spɪt], speak [spiːk].

[r], [ɹ] red, rich, rake, boar, care, tour

The correct IPA symbol for the typical English "r" is [ɹ], unless you mean the rolled Scottish [r]. However, the vast majority of English dictionaries denote the sound by [r] (and this book follows this convention). It never appears at the end of a standalone word in British English, but it is pronounced even in British English if it is immediately followed by another word beginning with a vowel. In this case, the [r] at the end is usually denoted by [ʳ] or [(r)] in dictionaries. For example, "boar" is pronounced [bɔːʳ] in British English, which means that "a boar sleeps" would be pronounced as [əˈbɔː ˈsliːps] whereas "a boar is" would be [əˈbɔːˈrɪz] (the [r] tends to be pronounced the beginning of the next syllable rather than where it is written).

[s] sit, soap, same, boss, kiss, house

Most people have no problem with the sound (but don't confuse it with [θ]), but the way it's written may be a source of confusion. It is usually represented by "s", "c", "sc", and "ss", but all of these can be pronounced also differently ("s" and "ss" as [z], "c" as [k], "sc" as [sk]) and there is no general rule which would help you decide which pronunciation is the correct one.

Nevertheless, you should remember that "-s" at the end of a word when it means the third person singular of a verb (e.g. "he goes") or a plural noun (e.g. "beds") is always pronounced as [z],

unless it follows an unvoiced consonant (e.g. "bets")—then it's pronounced as [s].

[ʃ] shy, shot, chef, posh, bush, douche

This sound is created by saying [s] but bending your tongue further to the upper palate. It is usually represented by "sh", but sometimes also by "ch", as in "chef", "machine", "niche".

[tʰ], [t] two, tall, tea, hot, bat, put

The very same rules about aspiration that hold for "k" and "p"
hold also for "t", i.e. it is always aspirated when it is at the beginning of a stressed syllable (two, tall, tea) and in many dialects also
almost everywhere else, except after "s" (e.g. step, still)

[ɾ] letter, better, written (Am. English only)

Where a Brit would say [tʰ], an American often says something
that sounds like a fast touch of [d]. It is called "alveolar flap" and is
usually represented by a double "t". However, many dictionaries ignore the distinction and denote it also by [t].

[tʃ] chat, China, choose, rich, catch, much

This sound sounds approximately like [t] and [ʃ] pronounced together. It is usually represented by "ch" or "tch" in writing, but "ch"
is also often pronounced [k] and sometimes [ʃ].

[v] van, very, vile, stove, leave, save

This sound is the "v" sound of most languages (also represented
by "w" in some, e.g. German and Polish). The letter "v" always represents the sound as in the words above, never [w] (as in "wow"). It
is also important to pronounce it as [v] and not as [f] also at the end
of a word; "leave" and "leaf" are not pronounced the same (although the difference is subtle).

[W] we, wow, wax, dwell, swine, twain

This sound must be distinguished from [v]; "wary" and "vary" don't sound the same. It never occurs at the end of a word, but may appear in the middle. It is usually represented by the letter "w".

[Z] zoo, xenon, zoom, is, has, booze

This sound usually causes few pronunciation problems, but the way it's written can be confusing. The letter "z" usually represents [z] (German speakers beware), but "x-" at the beginning of a word is also usually pronounced [z], and "s" at the end of a word is also often pronounced [z] if it is preceded by a vowel or a voiced consonant, but not always.

[ʒ] genre, version, measure, massage, equation

This sound is a softer version of [z]. It is usually represented by "s" in "-sion", "-sure", or by "g" in "-ge". As far as I know, there is only one English word which begins with this sound: "genre" [ˈʒɒn-rə] UK, [ˈʒɑːnrə] US.

III.2 Pronunciation of Vowels

As irregular as English orthography may be, there are still certain rules for pronunciation of vowels that don't form part of a larger letter group, and that's what this section will be about. The pronunciation is given in the IPA, as well as using an example in which the **stressed syllable** is bold and the vowel of which it is an <u>example</u> is underlined.

Pronunciation of vowels generally depends on two factors; whether it is stressed or not and whether it is in an open or a closed syllable (in writing, not in pronunciation). Here are the rules:

A	Stressed	Not stressed
Open	[eɪ] t<u>a</u>ke	[ə] syll<u>a</u>ble
Closed	[æ] c<u>a</u>t [ɑː] p<u>a</u>lm	[ɪ] char<u>a</u>cter [ə] pyjam<u>a</u>s

There is no reliable rule to decide when a in a closed stressed syllable is pronounced as [æ] and when as [ɑː], and this is also one of the biggest differences between American and British English (for example "grass" is pronounced [grɑːs] in the UK and [græs] in the US). Also, pay attention to the fact that there can be more than one stress in a word. For example, "pineapple" is pronounced ['paɪnˌæpl] with "a" being stressed as well, which causes it to be pronounced as [æ] rather than [ɪ] or [ə].

E	Stressed	Not stressed
Open	[iː] P<u>e</u>ter	[ɪ] <u>e</u>normous [i] sim<u>i</u>l<u>e</u>
Closed	[ɛ] g<u>e</u>t	[ə] mom<u>e</u>nt

The letter "e" plays a somewhat special role in English. Apart from its regular use (as in the table above), it is often used as a silent letter to make the previous syllable look like an open syllable. For example, in the word "take", the final "e" remains silent, but is used to make the word optically two-syllabic (i.e. *ta-ke*), thus changing the sound of a from [æ] to [eɪ].

I	Stressed	Not stressed
Open	[aj] p<u>i</u>ne	[ɪ] determ<u>i</u>ne [ə] terr<u>i</u>ble
Closed	[ɪ] p<u>i</u>t	[ɪ] rap<u>i</u>d

The case of the letter "I" is somewhat more complex, because it is generally hard to tell where the boundaries of syllables are, and this may be quite different also among various dialects of English. For example, "vitamin" is pronounced ['vaɪtəmɪn] in American English (and divided into syllables as vi-ta-min), whereas it is pronounced as ['vɪtəmɪn] in British English (and divided as vit-a-min correspondingly).

O	Stressed	Not stressed
Open	[əʊ] v<u>o</u>te [ʌ] c<u>o</u>me	[əʊ] cell<u>o</u> [ə] fel<u>o</u>ny
Closed	[ɒ], [ɑː] c<u>o</u>nscious	[ə] Cath<u>o</u>lic

The [ɒ] sound is used in British English whereas the [ɑː] sound is used in American English. There are two large classes of exceptions to the rules above. When "o" is followed by "r" in a stressed syllable, such as in "sport", "chord", "sore" etc., it is usually pronounced [ɔː] UK, [ɔːr] US. In many words whose last letter is a stressed "o", it is pronounced as [uː], such as in "do", "who", "two", "ado" etc. The words in which it is pronounced [ʌ] have to be learned by heart.

U	Stressed	Not stressed
Open	[uː], [juː] c<u>u</u>te	[uː], [juː] ind<u>u</u>ce
Closed	[ʌ] c<u>u</u>p	[ə] papyr<u>u</u>s

If "u" follows "r" or "l" in an open syllable, it is pronounced just [uː], such as in "crude", "prune", "Luke", "flu" etc. In American English, this happens also after other consonants, e.g. induce, duke, nuke whereas in British English, it is usually pronounced [juː] in such cases. When "u" is followed by "r" in a closed syllable, it is usually pronounced [ɜː] UK, [ɝː] US, e.g. curve, occur.

III.3 Letter groups in English

Among all the irregularities in English orthography, there are a few patterns of pronunciation that can be learned. Note: the rules described below hold only if the respective group lies within one syllable. For example, "ee" is always pronounced [iː], but not in "preemptive" [priˈɛmptɪv] (pree-**emp**-tiv), simply because the syllables are "pre-emp-tive" (resp. "pre-emp-ti-ve" according to orthographic rules), not "preemp-tive". Pronunciation in this section is given in British English unless stated otherwise.

"wh" as in **wh**ere, **wh**ich is usually taught to be pronounced just as [w] (i.e. that "**wh**ere" and "were", "**wh**ich" and "witch" sound the same), and indeed, this is the most common pronunciation. However, there are also many dialects in which it is pronounced as [hw], i.e with "h" front of "w"—Rowan Atkinson is a good example of this kind of pronunciation. Linguists also sometimes denote this sound by a separate symbol: [ʍ] (i.e. [ʍ] is pronounced as [hw]). There are a couple of words in which it is the "w" is silent, not "h", e.g. **wh**o, **wh**ole, **wh**ore (but not all that begin with "who" are of that kind, for example **wh**orl [wɜːl], **wh**oa [wəʊ].

"oo" is mostly pronounced in two different ways: [uː], as in f**oo**l, c**oo**l, or [ʊ], as in b**oo**k, l**oo**k (the same sound as in p**u**t, f**u**ll). There is no rule to decide which one is the correct one. It is sometimes pronounced also [ɔː] when written as "oor", as in d**oor**, fl**oor**, but the pronunciation differs among dialects (for example, there are many dialects in which "poor" is pronounced [pɔː] in the UK, [pɔːr] in the US, whereas in others it is pronounced with [ʊ]). There are also two words in which "oo" is pronounced [ʌ]: "bl**oo**d" and "fl**oo**d".

"ow" can be pronounced either [aʊ], as in c**ow**, h**ow**, or [əʊ] in British English resp. [ou] in American English, as in l**ow**, sn**ow**. There is no rule dictating when to use which one; there are even 4 words that can be pronounced both ways with different meanings: bow, row, sow, mow.

"ng" is usually pronounced as [ŋ], as in wrong, song. This is true even if it is followed by "ing", for example singing ['sɪŋɪŋ], longing ['lɒŋɪŋ], or by "er" when it means a person doing something, for example singer ['sɪŋəʳ], gunslinger ['gʌnslɪŋəʳ]. In other such cases, it is pronounced [ŋg], for example longer ("more long") ['lɒŋgəʳ], strongest [strɒŋgɪst]. It can also be [ŋk] when followed by "st", but there are only two such words: angst and amongst.

"nk" is pronounced [ŋk], as in think, blink. It must be pronounced with the "k" at the end in order to be distinguished from "ng"! "Think" and "thing" don't sound the same.

"ch" is mostly pronounced either as [k], as in character, chord, or as [tʃ], as in chicken, chest. Almost all words containing "chi" or "che" are pronounced with [tʃ] (but there are also a few exceptions, e.g. "chiropractor" ['kaɪərəʊpræktəʳ] and "chemistry" ['kɛmɪstri]), but there's no reliable rule for "cha", "cho", and "chu". In some words of French origin, it is pronounced as [ʃ] (sh), for example chef, chic.

"ps" is pronounced just as [s] (p is silent), for example psychology, psalm.

"eu" is pronounced as [uː] or [juː], as in neuter, leukaemia, and sometimes also short ([ʊ] or [jʊ]). The difference depends mostly on the dialect; it doesn't carry any difference in meaning ([uː] is used mostly in British English and [juː] in American English). Nevertheless, "eu" is generally just [uː] after "l" and "r".

"au" is pronounced as [ɔː], e.g. caution, aura.

"th" has two possible pronunciations: [θ], as in think, author, and [ð], as in that, although. There is no general rule to decide which one is the correct one.

"sh" is pronounced as [ʃ], as in show, fish.

"aw" is usually pronounced as [ɔ:], as in hawk, paw.

"ee" is pronounced as [i:], as in need, seen.

"ur", **"er"**, and **"ir"** are usually pronounced [ɜ:] UK [ɝ:] US, as in curve, purge, herd, serve, bird, stir.

That was it!

Thank you for reading this book; I hope you enjoyed the process of it. Several other books on issues English learners must face are currently under preparation, and a lot of freely available information can be found at

www.jakubmarian.com

You can also follow the author on

Facebook: http://www.facebook.com/JakubMarianOfficial

Google+: http://gplus.to/JakubMarian

Twitter: http://twitter.com/JakubMarian

Should you find any mistake in the book, or if you just think there is another word that should be included in the book, please, send me an email to

jakub.marian.errors@gmail.com

with the subject "English pronunciation".

Made in the USA
Lexington, KY
13 May 2015